TEACHING FOR Wisdom, Intelligence, Creativity, and Success

T0056843

TEACHING FOR Wisdom, Intelligence, Creativity, and Success

ROBERT J. STERNBERG
LINDA JARVIN
ELENA L. GRIGORENKO

Skyhorse Publishing

Contents

List of Tables

Preface

About This Book

This book aims to bring together some of the enduring themes and most significant work of Robert J. Sternberg and his collaborators at the Center for the Psychology of Abilities, Competencies, and Expertise (PACE), a center originally at Yale University and now at Tufts University. The book offers a rationale and suggestions for K–12 instruction and assessment based on Sternberg's theories, and the empirical work based on these theories, to foster in students the capacity for wise, successfully intelligent, and creative learning, problem solving, and living. This book represents an overview of roughly a dozen years of collaborations with teachers in different grade levels all across the United States and abroad. We are grateful to all the collaborators we have had over the years, and dedicate this book to the teachers with whom we have worked.

The book comprises five main parts, providing (1) an introduction, (2) a guide on how to teach for successful intelligence, (3) a guide on how to assess for successful intelligence, (4) a guide on how to teach and assess for wise thinking, and, finally, (5) a synthesis to show how you can bring it all together in your classroom. In each chapter, you will find an overview of the concepts (e.g., successful intelligence, principles for sound assessment, wisdom), followed by concrete, hands-on examples of how *you* can implement these ideas in your classroom. Each part ends with a "your turn" space for you to reflect on and apply what you have just learned in that part. Yes, we will put you to work and ask you to respond to the book!

We hope that you will find this book to be a helpful and inspiring resource.

Acknowledgments

Throughout this book, we have provided examples of learning and assessment activities sampled from a number of different curriculum units developed by the PACE Center in recent years. We are very grateful to all the PACE members who were involved in this effort, and wish to thank (in alphabetical order):

Damian Birney, Kathleen Connolly, Bill Disch, Tona Donlon, Niamh Doyle, Sarah Duman, Nancy Fredine, Carol Gordon, Pamela Hartman, Smaragda Kazi, Jonna Kwiatkowski, Jacqueline Leighton, Delci Lev, Donna Macomber, Nefeli Misuraca, Erik Moga, Tina Newman, Paul O'Keefe, Renate Otterbach, Carolyn Parish, Judi Randi, Morgen Reynolds, Alina Reznitskaya, Robyn Rissman, Christina Schwartz, Steven Stemler, Olga Stepanossova, Kristen Wendell, and Christopher Wright.

The work reflected in this book and the book's preparation was supported by several grants: Grants REC-9979843, REC-0710915, and REC-0633952 from the National Science Foundation, the College Board, and Educational Testing Services (ETS) through Contract PO # 0000004411, Grant Award # 31–1992–701 from the United States Department of Education, Institute for Educational Sciences (as administered by the Temple University Laboratory for Student Success), Grant R206R950001 under the Javits Act Program as administered by the Office of Educational Research and Improvement, U.S. Department of Education, and a grant from the W. T. Grant Foundation. Grantees undertaking such projects are encouraged to express freely their professional judgment. This book, therefore, does not necessarily represent the position or policies of the National Science Foundation, the College Board, Educational Testing Service, the United States Department of Education, or the W. T. Grant foundation and no official endorsement should be inferred.

The publisher gratefully acknowledges the contributions of the following individuals:

William E. Doll, Jr.
Emeritus Professor
Louisiana State University
Baton Rouge, LA

Daniel Elliott
Professor
Azusa Pacific University
Azusa, CA

Sharon Kane
Professor
State University of
   New York at Oswego
Oswego, NY

Susan Leeds
Science Educator
Howard Middle School
Orlando, FL

Phyllis Milne
Associate Director of Curriculum
   and Student Achievement
York County School Division
Yorktown, VA

James Morrison
Coordinator of
   Curriculum Development
University of Oklahoma,
   College of Liberal Studies
Norman, OK

Alcione Ostorga
Assistant Professor
University of Texas,
   Pan American
Edinburg, TX

Sue Pedro
Director of Elementary
   Curriculum and Instruction
Washington
   Local Schools
Toledo, OH

About the Authors

Robert J. Sternberg is Dean of the School of Arts and Sciences, Professor of Psychology, and Adjunct Professor of Education at Tufts University. He also is Honorary Professor of Psychology at the University of Heidelberg. Formerly, he was IBM Professor of Psychology and Professor of Management at Yale. At both Tufts and Yale, he has directed the Center for the Psychology of Abilities, Competencies, and Expertise. Dr. Sternberg's PhD is from Stanford and he holds ten honorary doctorates from ten different countries. In addition, he has won more than two dozen awards for his work. He is a former president of the American Psychological Association and Eastern Psychological Association, and he has authored over 1,200 books, articles, and book chapters.

Linda Jarvin is currently Associate Research Professor in Tufts University's Department of Education and the Deputy Director of Tufts's faculty development center (CELT). She received her PhD in Cognitive Psychology and Individual Differences from the University of Paris V (France), and completed her postdoctoral training at Yale University. Dr. Jarvin has led professional development workshops for hundreds of teachers across the United States, as well as in Europe and Africa.

Elena L. Grigorenko received her PhD in General Psychology from Moscow State University (Russia) in 1990, and her PhD in Developmental Psychology and Genetics from Yale University in 1996. Currently, Dr. Grigorenko is Associate Professor of Child Studies, Psychology, and Epidemiology and Public Health at Yale and Adjunct Professor of Psychology at Columbia University and Moscow State University

(Russia). Dr. Grigorenko has published more than 200 peer-reviewed articles, book chapters, and books. She has received many professional awards, and her research has been funded by various federal and private organizations. Dr. Grigorenko has worked with children from around the world, including those living in Africa, Asia, Europe, and the Americas.

PART I

Teaching for Wisdom, Intelligence, Creativity, and Success

Introduction to Teaching for Wisdom, Intelligence, Creativity, and Success

Part I briefly summarizes the theoretical model of human thinking and reasoning that we believe can provide insight into how students learn best. The theoretical model we refer to is known as "WICS" for Wisdom, Intelligence, and Creativity, Synthesized. We believe that wisdom, intelligence, and creativity are key ingredients in a successful person's life, and that it is very important in educational settings to help students build on all these skills, in other words, to synthesize them. If you want to learn more about the theory behind the model, we have included an annotated bibliography of articles and books that describe the model more in detail in the Appendix to Part I at the end of this book. There, you will also find references to other authors who have investigated how students learn and offer strategies for teaching different skills such as analysis and creativity in the classroom.

Here we will just briefly review the WICS model, present some arguments for the importance of teaching for intelligence, creativity, and wisdom in the K–12 classroom, and finally, provide a brief self-evaluation scale for you, the reader, to determine your own profile of skills: Are your main strengths in memory, analytical, practical, or creative abilities, or in some combination of them? A scoring key is provided in Answer Key toward the end of the book.

Figure 1.1 gives a visual overview of the WICS model.

Figure 1.1   TheWICS Model of Thinking

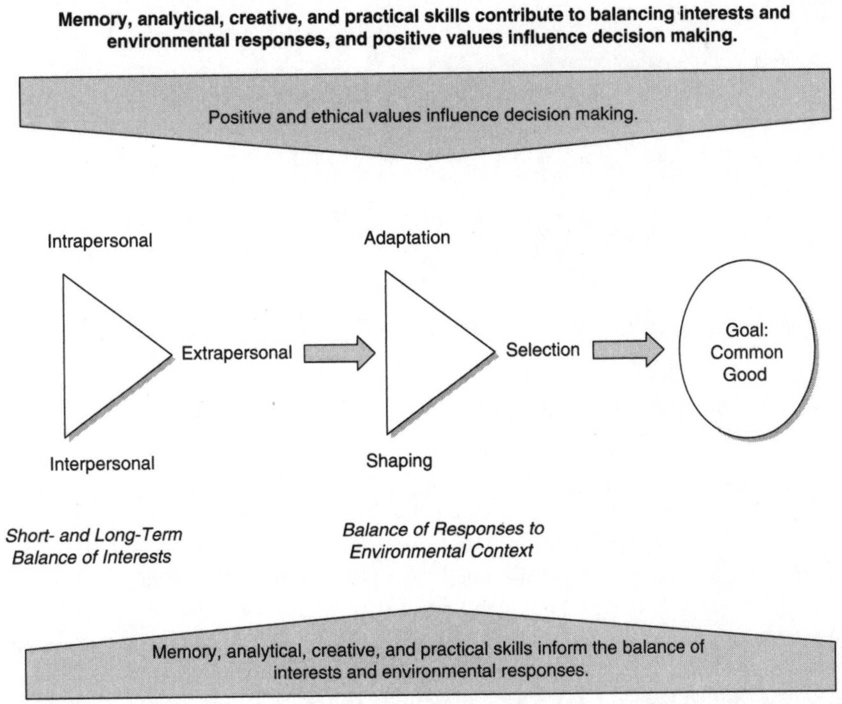

Memory, analytical, creative, and practical skills contribute to balancing interests and environmental responses, and positive values influence decision making.

Positive and ethical values influence decision making.

Intrapersonal

Adaptation

Extrapersonal

Selection

Goal: Common Good

Interpersonal

Shaping

Short- and Long-Term Balance of Interests

Balance of Responses to Environmental Context

Memory, analytical, creative, and practical skills inform the balance of interests and environmental responses.

What Is the WICS Model?

The purpose of this book is to serve as a hands-on guide to inspire you to broaden your teaching and assessment repertoire to ensure that all students in your classroom are as successful as they can be. The goal is not to offer you an Introductory Psychology or Intelligence 101 course, but to provide you with suggestions for dealing with some practical and real situations in the classroom.

Before we start, however, we quickly summarize the different theories of intelligence that are in vogue and describe the one we subscribe to, so that you know our position and so that we're all on the same page. In a nutshell, there are two kinds of theories of intelligence: (1) the single-faceted, unified general intelligence (or *g*-factor) theories, which emphasize the nature of intelligence as a single entity; and (2) the multifaceted conceptions of intelligence, which emphasize the importance of multiple and distinctive aspects of intelligence.

Those who think that the first type of theory is correct generally view intelligence as relatively fixed and predetermined by genetic endowment, and as relatively independent from schooling. In other words, according to this theory, you are born with a certain amount of smarts, and the type of schooling you receive won't change it that much. The authors of this book, however, subscribe to the second of these two conceptions of intelligence. Many researchers who are familiar to teachers subscribe to this view, for example, Howard Gardner, the author of the theory of Multiple Intelligences. Investigators in the second group generally agree that intelligence is the flexible capacity to learn from experience and to adapt to one's environment (using the skills required by and acquired through a specific cultural and social context). They also tend to agree that intelligence can be developed, whether through formal explicit instruction or in informal educational situations (depending on the types of abilities considered). The authors of this book believe that everyone has some initial abilities, and that these can be developed into competencies, and that these competencies can in turn be honed into expertise. We believe that these initial abilities depend in part on genetic heritage, but the manner and degree to which this genetic endowment is realized depends on the individual's environment. We believe that the key to success in the classroom—and in life more broadly—lies in a combination of intelligence, creativity, and wisdom, as per the WICS model.

We also believe there is an urgent need to teach to all abilities, and to match the assessment of achievement to such broad teaching. The time has come to capitalize on the variety of human resources because students' talents do not happen to correspond to the skills that schools traditionally have emphasized. Creative and practical abilities are certainly as important in life as are memory and analytical abilities, and they can be as important in school if a school chooses to emphasize these abilities. The next parts of this book will provide you with more details on how to teach and assess for a broader range of abilities, and give you a wealth of concrete examples from classrooms at different grade levels and in different content areas.

Let's say that, so far, you agree with us that, in order to succeed in life, students need more than rote memorization and the ability to analyze. Let's say, also, that you think teachers should promote a broader range of skills in their classrooms to help more students of different abilities and learning profiles to succeed. At the same time, you may be asking yourself whether it's worth trying to implement all these changes and broaden your teaching repertoire. Teachers today are under a lot of pressure and have many constraints related to seeing their students perform well on tests. Indeed, many teachers we have worked with over the years say that although they would like to include more creative activities in their classroom, for example, their school administration is not supportive and emphasizes only the importance of test scores. We all want to promote high achievement in our students, and we think that by broadening your teaching repertoire and addressing the needs of a wider range of students with different learning styles, you will do exactly that. You will help students—*all* students—achieve at higher levels. Teaching for creativity is not just a nice and fun add-on to the regular curriculum. On the contrary, it is a means to teach content, the content that our local, state, and federal standards and scope and sequence guidelines ask us to teach. In the Appendix to Part I at the end of this book, you'll find references to studies where we have actually measured whether or not this approach promotes learning (it does!), but for now, let's just list the four main reasons why the WICS model works for students and teachers.

REASON #1: APPRECIATION OF DIFFERENCES

To teach within the WICS model is to create a supportive learning environment in which students find their own ability patterns, understand how uniqueness allows each individual to make a particular contribution to the learning community, and value diversity. One step toward this goal is to *balance* the types of activities you offer your students so as to broaden the range of abilities addressed and give more students a chance to capitalize on their strengths (and compensate for their weaknesses). Part III of this book will give you some charts to help you achieve this balance in your classroom.

REASON #2: INCREASING RETENTION OF THE MATERIALS LEARNED

When you teach students through analytical, creative, as well as practical instruction, you enable students to encode information in three different ways (analytically, creatively, and practically), in addition to encoding it for memory. Multiple encodings of information can help improve learning. The portion of this book devoted to teaching for enhancing memory will tell you more about how our memory works.

REASON #3: BUILDING ON STRENGTHS

In a classroom where only one type of skill is addressed (memorization, for example), only one type of learner, memory learners, will feel that they are able to use their strengths to be successful. Students who have strengths in other areas (creativity, for example) will never be able to let those strengths shine in the classroom. If, in contrast, you teach for a broad range of skills, you will give all students a chance to capitalize on their strengths and to compensate for, or correct, their weaknesses. In other words, there should be at least some instruction that is compatible with almost all students' strengths, enabling students to bring these strengths to bear on the work at hand. Instruction that enables students to capitalize on their strengths is also more likely to motivate students. At the same time, at least some of the instruction will probably not correspond to students' strengths. It is important also to encourage students to develop modes of compensation for and correction of weaknesses.

REASON #4: INCREASING STUDENT MOTIVATION

Instruction that balances different types of activities addressing different students' strengths (memory, analytical, creative, practical, and wise thinking skills) will be more motivating to students simply because it makes the material to be learned more interesting. Indeed, when we ask students whose teachers apply the WICS model about their engagement in the curriculum material, we find WICS-based instruction to be effective in capturing the students' interest. And, we all know that school today competes with a variety of different environmental stimulants and capturing attention of students is difficult, so having a pedagogy that appears to be able to do so is really important for the overall success of schooling.

Your Turn

What Is Your Pattern of Strengths?

Now that we have reviewed the different types of abilities the WICS model focuses on, let's explore your own pattern of strengths, imagining that you are a student. Below, you will find a series of questions about your preferred assessments. This is not a scientific "test"; it's just one way to start thinking about your own preferred mode(s) of thinking, so that you can keep it in mind when you read the rest of the book and consider your students' varying patterns of strengths. We are intentionally putting you in a student's shoes, because typically students are not asked any of these questions because they are not usually given choices similar to those presented below. But, if you find yourself having preferences, so might they! Ready? Let's go! When you are finished, look at the answer key on page 13.

For each of the questions below, rate on a scale from 1 (low) to 5 (high) how much you would enjoy being evaluated via each type of assessment. You can use the same rating (1–5) several times for a give question. We're interested in your preferences, not in how easy each assessment would be. For example, it might be quicker to answer multiple-choice questions, but you would really more enjoy doing a project. For all these questions, please assume that you have studied the topics and know something about them, even if in reality you don't know anything about soccer and wouldn't know how to compare it to football.

1. You just studied a lesson on the history of the Civil War.

I'd like to be evaluated with a(n)	Your rating (1–5)
a. multiple-choice test	
b. essay test asking me to compare the Civil War to the American Revolution	
c. test asking me to create an imaginary soldier and then write a fictionalized story that is nevertheless true to the details of the war, describing the soldier's life during the course of the war	
d. essay question asking me what lessons the Civil War holds for resolving the polarization between liberals and conservatives in contemporary American society	

2. You have just learned how to compute areas of different types of polygons.

I'd like to be evaluated with a(n)	Your rating (1–5)
a. test where I describe from memory how to compute the areas of each of the types of polygons	
b. test containing mathematical word problems that involve my computing areas of polygons in the context of solving the problems	
c. test where I have to write the mathematical word problems involving computing areas of polygons	
d. test where I compute the approximate area of the town in which I live, given a to-scale map	

3. You have just read the novel *Tom Sawyer*.

I'd like to be evaluated with a(n)	Your rating (1–5)
a. multiple-choice test requiring me to remember people and events from the book.	
b. test asking me to analyze how Tom Sawyer and Huck Finn are similar and different as people	

(Continued)

(Continued)

I'd like to be evaluated with a(n)	Your rating (1–5)
c. prompt to write a short story about what happened to Tom Sawyer and Becky Thatcher ten years later	
d. prompt to write an analysis of lessons about persuasion and salesmanship to be learned from Tom Sawyer's convincing his friends to whitewash Aunt Polly's fence	

4. You have just studied a biological-science lesson on the functioning of the major organs of the human body.

I'd like to be evaluated with a(n)	Your rating (1–5)
a. fill-in-the-blanks test assessing my mastery of the different functions of the major organs	
b. essay on how the functioning of the brain can affect the functioning of the heart	
c. assessment involving designing an experiment to see how different stressors affect the functioning of the heart	
d. essay on how smoking damages the functioning of the lungs	

5. You have just studied the geography of the Alps mountain range.

I'd like to be evaluated with a(n)	Your rating (1–5)
a. multiple-choice test assessing my knowledge of the geography of the Alps	
b. assessment asking me to compare the geography of the Alps to that of the Andes	
c. written task involving writing a story about the geography of a mountain range on an imaginary planet	
d. essay showing how the geography of the Alps has helped to promote alpine tourism	

6. In Spanish class, you have just learned words for many different kinds of foods.

I'd like to be evaluated with a(n)	Your rating (1–5)
a. fill-in-the-blanks test assessing my recall of the Spanish equivalents of the English words for ten different kinds of foods	
b. prompt to write an essay showing how the Spanish and English words for different kinds of foods are similar and different, and what generalizations can be drawn from these similarities and differences	
c. task involving creating an imaginary dialogue between an American diner and a Spanish waiter, where the American orders food in Spanish	
d. prompt to write an essay in Spanish on the healthiness of several different kinds of foods served in restaurants	

7. In art class, you have just studied principles of perspective in drawing and painting.

I'd like to be evaluated with a(n)	Your rating (1–5)
a. fill-in-the-blanks test assessing my memory for the principles	
b. assessment asking me to compare the use of perspective by two painters, Bosch and Bruegel	
c. task requiring the drawing of a scene in a park using the principles of perspective I learned	
d. demonstration of how principles of perspective are applied in a modern building in the town in which I live	

8. In music class, you have studied some principles of harmony.

I'd like to be evaluated with a	Your rating (1–5)
a. multiple-choice test on the principles of harmony	
b. prompt to compare the use of principles of harmony by Beethoven versus Copeland	

(Continued)

(Continued)

I'd like to be evaluated with a	Your rating (1–5)
c. task to compose a tune in which I use principles of harmony	
d. prompt asking me to demonstrate how principles of harmony are used in contemporary advertising jingles to make products appealing to consumers	

9. In physical education, you have learned the rules of soccer.

I'd like to be evaluated with a(n)	Your rating (1–5)
a. fill-in-the-blanks test on the rules of soccer	
b. prompt to compare and contrast the rules of American football with soccer	
c. prompt to create my own game that is a combination of American football and soccer	
d. assessment asking me to demonstrate how violations of soccer rules were responsible for the defeat of a particular team in a recent World Cup match	

10. In general, to what extent do you prefer each of the following?

I'd like to be evaluated with a(n)	Your rating (1–5)
a. multiple-choice tests assessing my memory of material I have learned	
b. analytical essay test that requires me to analyze, compare and contrast, or evaluate things or ideas	
c. project where I have free reign for deciding how creatively to study a topic	
d. practical assessment that requires me to apply what I have learned to a real-world problem	

We hope you enjoyed completing the survey!

To score, add up the numbers you have written down for all the As, Bs, Cs, and Ds. You can use the table below to do it:

Question number	Rating for option A	Rating for option B	Rating for option C	Rating for option D
1				
2				
3				
4				
5				
6				
7				
8				
9				
10				
Total				

What do these scores mean? The response items labeled A are memory-based; the Bs, analytically-based; the Cs, creatively-based; and the Ds, practically-based. Your relative scores should give you a sense of your preference for each of the kinds of activities. In other words, if you score higher on A than on C, it indicates that you prefer to complete assessments that draw mostly on your memory skills rather than to complete assessments that ask you to be creative.

Notice that, in this particular assessment, we are looking at your preferences, and not necessarily your skills, for the different kinds of tasks you might confront.

Some of us have a clear preference for one type of activity or skill (always practical, for example), while some of us tend to like all types of activities and no clear preference stands out.

Are you surprised by your results, or are these results what you expected?

Now think about what implications this exercise can have for your classroom. Your students have both preferences and profiles of success that can be very different from yours. If you teach and assess only to one type of ability (the one you prefer, say), then students with different profiles of strengths and preferences will have very few opportunities to shine in your classroom.

In the rest of this book, we will discuss how you can make sure that you address the needs of a broad range of students in your classroom, while at the same time making sure that you develop wise thinking skills in your students as well.

PART II

Why and How to Teach for Successful Intelligence

Introduction to Teaching for Successful Intelligence

If you walk into a typical classroom, one thing you will notice right away is that students come in all sizes, shapes, and forms—they are all very different from one another. And once you start teaching them, you discover that it's not just their physical appearance, but also their ways of learning and engaging in the classroom that are different. Some students are more engaged when they get to participate in hands-on activities, such as in a science lab. Other students are happiest when left alone in a corner reading or writing. Some pupils do well orally in one-on-one interactions with you or with their peers, but if you ask them to express themselves in writing, they do poorly. Some pupils do well with numbers, others with graphs and schematic representations, while some others do better with words to make meaning of numerical concepts.

Different students (and different teachers!) learn in different ways. To help us think about different types of students, consider how they learn best. As part of this consideration, offer students activities that will allow them to capitalize on their strengths, as well as activities that will help them reinforce their skills in areas in which they are not as proficient. Four main sets of skills are particularly relevant to reaching all students: memory, analytical (or critical) thinking, creative thinking, and practical thinking. Let's illustrate with a classroom description:

Shayna is a fourth grader with very strong analytical skills: she can read a story and quickly analyze the plot, determining the key elements of the story. But when it comes to displaying creative skills and writing a story of her own, she has difficulty coming up with original ideas. Taylor, on the other hand, is very creative: his creative abilities are not limited to story writing; he also displays these creative skills in science, and is usually the first student in the class to come up with ideas for new experiments. Ana represents yet a different pattern of strengths. When, in mathematics, she is given an abstract fraction problem to solve (such as 1/6 x 3), she is lost; but, if the problem is put into a concrete context so that she can see the practical consequences (for example, by asking her to divide three candy bars equally among six friends), she can solve the problem. Her practical abilities also shine through in language arts projects (for example, when students are asked to search for information on a given topic and present it to the rest of the class).

Take a moment to think about your own classroom. Can you think of students with these different profiles of strengths? If you are not presently in a classroom, think about your friends, family members, or peers to complete this reflection. Try to think of a specific activity or assignment in which each one of these students shines.

A student in my class who displays good memory skills is_____.

S/he likes to ☐ memorize ☐ recall ☐ recite

☐ (*Think of your own example here*)

_____

_____

_____

_____

A student in my class who displays good analytical skills is_____.

S/he likes to ☐ compare & contrast ☐ analyze ☐ evaluate
☐ explain ☐ judge ☐ critique

☐ (*Think of your own example here*)

_____

_____

_____

_____

A student in my class who displays good creative skills is_____.

S/he likes to ☐ create ☐ design ☐ invent ☐ imagine ☐ suppose

☐ (*Think of your own example here*)

_____

_____

_____

_____

A student in my class who displays good practical skills is_____.

S/he likes to ☐ apply ☐ implement ☐ employ ☐ contextualize

☐ (*Think of your own example here*)

_____

_____

_____

_____

The next four chapters explain how *any* curriculum can be infused with the featured skill, and providing examples from existing curriculum units at the elementary, middle, and high school levels. All the sample activities have been implemented and tested in classrooms.

How to Enhance Memory Skills

To teach for successful intelligence is to address four types of different thinking skills: memory, analytical skills, creative skills, and practical skills. Let's review each one of them and see how they can be enhanced. We start with memory because if you have no information or skills to draw upon, there is nothing to analyze, create, or apply!

One essential skill that we all have and use every day is memory. And, as most of us have experienced, memory fluctuates; some days you feel like you have much stronger memory skills than other days. Moreover, some people seem to have more of it than others. In healthy people, memory is like a muscle. It can be enhanced by giving it a regular "workout." Before we describe some of the strategies that can help your students (and you) enhance your memory skills, let's first review very briefly what memory is.

The three key elements to memory are: (1) encoding information (e.g., "getting it into your head"), (2) storing the information, and (3) retrieving the information effectively when you need it again. These skills are essential to success in life, in general, and in school, in particular. The skills are also important for high performance on standardized tests. Without memory—without something in our head to reason about—the other types of skills (analytical, practical, creative) are meaningless. You need information to analyze, to apply, or to be creative about and take to the next step. As the ancient Greek philosopher Plato is quoted as saying in the fourth century B.C., "All knowledge is but remembrance."

Since Plato, we've come a long way in understanding what the different components of memory are, and how we can enhance them. Research on memory continues to be a burgeoning field, both within psychology and in the new neuroscience disciplines. We will not go into much detail on this research here, but for those of you who are interested in learning more, you can consult a psychology textbook or one of the numerous books available on how to increase your memory. For now, we will just focus on the *encoding* and *retrieval* of information.

Encoding refers to the way in which the new information is placed into and then organized in memory. For example, it is more efficient to summarize information before putting it into memory, or to encode the same piece of information twice in two different ways, for example, by remembering a word and its corresponding image. Think of an everyday example: when you try to memorize a phone number, it is easier if you chunk it into groups of two or three digits, rather than remembering each single digit. Take your area code, for example. Do you think of it as a three-digit number or as three separate digits?

Retrieval refers to the way in which the information is sought and found in memory. It is how you find your way back to the mental "shelf" where you stored the information. It is easier to retrieve information that is interconnected with other information, so that there are several "clues" to retrieval.

How can we help students enhance their encoding of new information so that it is easier to retrieve? Research has shown that *multiple* and *diverse* encodings are preferable to a single encoding. Repetition is good! In terms of schooling, this means that it is better to give students several opportunities to study and review the same material. Ideally, the opportunities would be different in kind, to encourage diverse encodings. Another general rule is the "spacing effect." Reviews that are spaced out are better than reviews that are close together in time, despite what your students who cram the night before an exam might think. So, repetition is good but repetition with breaks in between is even better. Finally, the use of memory techniques (so called "mnemonic devices") is beneficial. In the classroom, you should give students a chance to practice both encoding and retrieval of information with specific mnemonic techniques.

Now that we've briefly reviewed the research, let's look at an example and put you to the test!

1. Take a piece of paper and a stopwatch or a watch that shows seconds.

2. When you are ready, look at the following number for ten seconds; then close the book and try to write down the number you just saw on your paper. You should not start writing down the number until *after* you've closed the book.

11231302928527246060

3. OK, now compare the number you wrote down to the number above. How many digits did you remember? Chances are, you did not remember all twenty digits. Now refer to the Answer Key at the end of this book and we'll illustrate how memory techniques could have helped you remember more digits.

In the Appendix to Part II, you will find more information on some specific mnemonic techniques and strategies that you can use in your daily life, or teach students to use. You will also find examples of classroom activities designed to enhance students' memory skills.

6 How to Enhance Analytical Skills

Most teachers provide instruction and learning experiences that require students to think analytically. Analytical skills are also sometimes referred to as critical thinking skills. Teaching for successful intelligence incorporates many instructional features that teachers typically use. Our aim is not to tell you about something radically new as much as it is to help you find a balance and make sure that all thinking skills can be proportionally represented throughout the curriculum. It is likely that in your classroom, analytical thinking is emphasized over practical or creative thinking most of the time, and you will not find it too difficult to come up with examples of analytical activities for your students. Below we provide some examples for inspiration.

LANGUAGE ARTS

The following are language arts skills that are essentially analytical in nature. (Please fill in the blanks with your own example.)

- Compare and contrast characters, plots, settings, or word meanings.
  _____
  _____
  _____

- Sequence or organize sentences, paragraphs, or events in a narrative.

  _____

  _____

  _____

- Differentiate fact from opinion or literary genres. _____

  _____

  _____

  _____

- Give an opinion of/evaluate a book, an idea, different reference
  sources, or your own work. _____

  _____

  _____

  _____

- Use context clues to infer the meaning of a new vocabulary word,
  or learn about a literary character. _____

  _____

  _____

  _____

- Identify cause and effect. _____

  _____

  _____

  _____

Many other instructional strategies require analytical thinking. For example, "word sorts" are commonly used to encourage students to identify and classify word patterns. In word sorts, students group together words that have the same spelling patterns, definitions, phonetic sounds, roots or affixes, and so forth. The word-sort concept can be extended to the study of literature; students can be asked to categorize types of characters, plot structures, and other literary elements. Another instructional strategy often used to help students categorize information is the advanced organizer. Graphic organizers such as semantic maps, flow charts, or Venn diagrams require analytical thinking.

Tables 1 and 2 present more examples of analytical language arts activities: one in which students analyze sentences to find the missing word and then combine clues to find the solution to a problem, and one in which groups of students compare and contrast different points of view.

Table 1   Analytical Activity From an Elementary School Lesson on the Mystery Genre

---

ACTIVITY: Solve it!

Student Identifier_____ Date_____

In this activity, you will discover the meanings of new words by solving a puzzle. Find a word in the box that matches each definition. Write the correct word next to its definition. Write one letter on a line. (Clues: The spaces tell you how many letters the word has.) Then write the numbered letters on the matching numbered lines at the bottom of the page. Your answer will tell you "Who solves the mystery?" You may use a dictionary to check your answers.

> mysterious, clue, villain, case, sleuth, suspect, witness, red herring, suspense, solution, evidence

1. Someone who solves mysteries; a detective ____ ____ ____ ____ ____ ____
                                 1

2. A hint that helps you solve the mystery ____ ____ ____ ____
                  2   3

3. An evil person; someone who commits a crime ____ ____ ____ ____ ____ ____ ____
                      4

4. Difficult to understand; puzzling ____ ____ ____ ____ ____ ____ ____ ____ ____
            5   6

5. Someone who sees something ____ ____ ____ ____ ____ ____ ____
                    7

6. Excitement from uncertainty; anticipation ____ ____ ____ ____ ____ ____ ____ ____
                  8

7. Someone people think committed the crime ____ ____ ____ ____ ____ ____ ____
                    9

8. A false clue; a clue that does not lead to the solution (two words)

____ ____ ____   ____ ____ ____ ____ ____ ____ ____
   10

9. The mystery to be solved ____ ____ ____ ____
      11

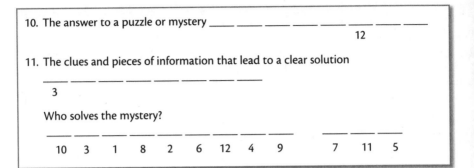

10. The answer to a puzzle or mystery ____ ____ ____ ____ ____ ____ ____ ____

12

11. The clues and pieces of information that lead to a clear solution

    ____ ____ ____ ____ ____ ____ ____ ____

3

    Who solves the mystery?

    ____ ____ ____ ____ ____ ____ ____ ____ ____   ____ ____ ____

10   3   1   8   2   6   12   4   9   7   11   5

Table 2   Analytical Activity From a High School Lesson Accompanying the Reading of H. G. Wells's *The Island of Dr. Moreau*

Group Activity (30 minutes):

Discuss the fight between the captain and Montgomery described in the opening chapter.

Divide the whole class into two teams. Within each team, make subgroups of three or four students. Ask one team to consider the captain's point of view, and the other team to take Montgomery's standpoint. Ask each subgroup to develop arguments showing that "their" side is right. Then have one representative from a "Captain group" and one representative from a "Montgomery group" come up and debate in front of the class. Repeat with all subgroups.

SCIENCE

The following are science skills that are essentially analytical in nature. (Please fill in the blanks with your own example.)

- Compare and contrast a concave and a convex lens, herbivores and carnivores, or temperatures expressed in degrees Fahrenheit vs. in degrees Celsius. _____

  _____

  _____

  _____

- Sequence or organize chemical elements, or different types of magnets.

  _____

  _____

  _____

  _____

- Interpret the results of an experiment or a phenomenon you observe in nature. _____

  _____

  _____

  _____

- Make and verify predictions. _____

  _____

  _____

  _____

- Critique the adequacy of a given experiment to test hypotheses or an author's interpretation of results. _____

  _____

  _____

  _____

- Identify cause and effect or different theoretical frameworks.

  _____

  _____

  _____

  _____

Many other instructional strategies require analytical thinking, such as making and verifying predictions or interpreting observational data. For example, a typical activity in an ecology unit might be to plant seeds and then measure how much the plant grows every two days, recording and interpreting the data. Representing these data graphically also requires analytical thinking.

Tables 3 and 4 present more examples of analytical science activities.

Table 3 Analytical Activity From an Elementary School Lesson on Properties of Materials

Activity:

- Distribute one set of the ten sorting objects (paper clip, aluminum foil, LEGO brick, plastic spoon or cap, index card, paper napkin, pencil, stick, band, and eraser) to each student pair. Ask students to sort the objects into groups that contain objects that are alike in some way. Give some examples: the spoon and the foil might be grouped because they are usually found in the kitchen; the foil and the index card might be grouped because they are both flat.
- While students are sorting, sort your own set of objects into five different groups according to their material type: metal (paper clip and aluminum), plastic (LEGO and spoon or cap), paper (card and napkin), wood (pencil and stick), and rubber (band and eraser).
- Allow five to ten minutes for sorting by student pairs. Students should describe their sorting method in their journals.

> Objects in group:
>
>
> How they are alike:

- Gather students together and ask each pair to tell the class about one of their object groups. As they describe their groups, record on a class chart their method for sorting. Divide the chart into three areas, one for sorting by property, one for sorting by function (use), and one for sorting by material type (but do not label these columns yet). For example, if students make a group of objects that are all white, record the word "white" on the chart in the property area.

If no student pair describes a group that is sorted by material (e.g., these items are all wood), then display your five groups and ask students to guess your sorting method. Record the five different material types on your class chart.

Table 4 Analytical Activity From a High School Physics Lesson on Atoms

Name:

Homework Sheet: Net Charges

The electrical charge of an atom depends on the balance between protons and electrons. Below you will find a description of four different collections of subatomic particles.

Find the net charge for each one of the subatomic particles:

Protons	Neutrons	Electrons	Charge
1	0	1	
1	4	2	
14	15	13	
11	3	12	

In the above example, you were given the number of protons, neutrons, and electrons and asked to find the net charge of each collection. Now you will be given the net charge, and your task is to make up a corresponding collection of subatomic particles.

Protons	Neutrons	Electrons	Charge
			−3
			+5
			0
			+6

MATHEMATICS

The following mathematics skills are essentially analytical in nature. (Please fill in the blanks with your own example.)

- Compare and contrast numbers greater and less than 2^2, or different solutions to a mathematical problem. _____

  _____

  _____

  _____

- Sequence or organize number patterns, or geometrical shapes.

  _____

  _____

  _____

  _____

- Identify and classify mathematical formulas or types of functions.

  _____

  _____

  _____

  _____

- Evaluate strategies for word problems or proofs. _____

  _____

  _____

  _____

- Estimate measurements or projections. _____

  _____

  _____

  _____

In addition to these mathematics skills, many teachers routinely employ instructional strategies that require analytical thinking. For example, asking students to solve problems and explain how they arrived at their solutions is commonly used to encourage students to analyze, reflect, and understand their reasoning. Another instructional strategy often used to help students categorize information is graphs. Students are asked to collect data and organize them using bar graphs, pie graphs, or line graphs. Determining the best type of graph to represent the data and organizing the data into categories to be represented requires analytical thinking.

Tables 5 and 6 present further examples of analytical math activities.

Table 5   Analytical Activity From an Elementary School Lesson on Number Sense and Place Value

Activity:

1. Order each set of numbers from greatest to least.
    9,635   7,891   10,568   11,456

    _____   _____   _____   _____

2. 99,765   44,567   100,456   45,600

    _____   _____   _____   _____

3. Order each set of numbers from least to greatest.
    7,899 755 7,567 70,733

    _____   _____   _____   _____

    100 156,700 122,455 105

    _____   _____   _____   _____

4. Use < or > or = to show the relationship between each pair of numbers.

    665 ⬭ 667   1,867 ⬭ 1,100

    39 ⬭ 139   10,546 ⬭ 10,546

Table 6   Analytical Activity From a High School Lesson on the Statistical Concepts of Mean, Median, and Mode

Student Instructions (divided in groups):

Imagine that you and your classmates have decided to organize a class trip to Boston. You survey students in the class to find out how much they are able to pay for the trip, and you find that the average amount of money that students were prepared to pay was $80. The school manages to negotiate a deal and the whole trip, all expenses included, will cost $78 per person. Do you think it's a good deal? Why or why not?

_____

_____

_____

_____

Now let's look at the answers to that questionnaire to see how much each student is prepared to pay.

Student 1: $40	Student 5: $140	Student 9: $40	Student 13: $40
Student 2: $90	Student 6: $40	Student 10: $40	Student 14: $90
Student 3: $40	Student 7: $80	Student 11: $40	Student 15: $80
Student 4: $100	Student 8: $80	Student 12: $300	Student 16: $40

Now, what do you think about the deal the school has negotiated? Is it a good deal? Why or why not?

_____

_____

_____

_____

SOCIAL SCIENCES

The following activities in social sciences are essentially analytical in nature. (Please fill in the blanks with your own example.)

- Compare and contrast two forms of government or two countries' foreign policy positions on a given issue. _____

  _____

  _____

  _____

- Sequence or organize historical events chronologically, or psychological theories of cognitive development. _____

  _____

  _____

  _____

- Identify and classify political figures' statements based on their ideology or historical buildings based on their styles of construction.

  _____

  _____

  _____

  _____

- Evaluate the historical impact of a given event or the financial cost of implementing a given social reform. _____

_____

_____

_____

Tables 7 and 8 further illustrate how you can strengthen students' analytical skills in the social sciences.

Table 7 Analytical Activity From a High School Lesson on Psychology (and the concept of rationalization, in particular)

Name:

Worksheet: Rationalization

In the text, the author describes rationalization as the ability to cope with feelings by reasoning about them. The author gives the example of someone who has failed a test and, thinking about it, realizes it was because he/she was thinking about something else. Think of another situation in everyday life where you will cope with your initial feelings by rationalizing. Describe the situation, your initial feelings, and then the possible logical reasons for what happened.

Situation:

_____

_____

_____

_____

Feelings:

_____

_____

_____

_____

Explanations:

_____

_____

_____

_____

Table 8   Analytical Activity From a Middle School Lesson on Conflict Resolution

---

Solving Dilemmas: Useful Questions

1. Who is involved in this dilemma?
   a. Main individual or group:

   _____

   _____

   _____

   b. Other individuals or groups:

   _____

   _____

   _____

2. What are the interests, points of view, or deeper goals and concerns of the individual or groups involved in the situation?
   a. Interests of main individual or group identified in question 1:

   _____

   _____

   _____

   b. Interests of other individual or group identified in question 1:

   _____

   _____

   _____

3. What are the values or principles deemed important by the main individual or group solving the dilemma?

   _____

   _____

   _____

4. Identify the desired result that is shared by everyone involved. What is the "common good" for all involved that the main individual or group should work toward?

   _____

   _____

   _____

(Continued)

Table 8 (Continued)

5. List two or more possible and realistic responses to the dilemma.

_____

_____

_____

6. Which of the responses listed above is the best response, and why?

_____

_____

_____

CLOSING ACTIVITY

Now think of an analytical activity in which you like to engage your students—or future students if you are not currently in a classroom. Describe the activity and explain why it mostly engages analytical skills. (Yes, this is an analytical activity in itself!)

Activity

_____

_____

_____

_____

Explanation

_____

_____

_____

_____

How to Enhance Creative Skills

When you hear the words "creativity" and "classroom," what is your first association? Chances are that you, like many teachers and parents, will think "art class." It is true that it takes creativity to paint, sculpt, or make a collage. It also takes creativity to write a poem or a short story, however, or to figure out how to communicate with a new student in school who does not speak the same language as you. What about coming up with a new hypothesis in science or an idea for a product or service that can grow into a business? That's right, these activities also require creativity. Creativity is not only what enables us to come up with new ideas (whatever the field); it is also the skill that enables us to deal with new situations or problems that we have never confronted before. In school, we often use "problem sets" with a predetermined set of correct answers, but in life most real-world problems come without a handy answer key, so creative skills are very important. Below are some examples of classroom activities designed to strengthen students' creative skills.

LANGUAGE ARTS

When language arts teachers think of creative learning experiences, the type of task that typically comes to mind is creative writing. Analytical, creative, and practical instruction, however, includes many other types of learning experiences intended to develop students' creative thinking. Reading can develop creativity. For example, when students predict a story's plot line, they are using creative thinking. You might encourage students to interact with the text as they read by imagining what they might say to a character or imagining what a character might do differently. Or you can introduce students to the idea of fan fiction, the increasingly popular practice of writing works of fiction about fictional characters created by others. For example, there are now many stories written about Harry Potter that do not come from the original author of the series. Vocabulary can provide another avenue for creative thinking. For example, students can coin words or invent new idioms.

Even concepts that are typically thought of as analytical, such as organizing for writing, can be given creative license. Encourage students to invent new ways of organizing. In one language arts unit targeting library research skills, students created a "trail" of sources by taking notes on color-coded "post-it" notes that marked page references. Most library research projects culminate in a "report." Consider, however, asking your students to present their information in different ways. Asking students to brainstorm unusual ways to demonstrate what they have learned provides another creative learning experience.

The following language arts skills are essentially creative in nature. (Please fill in the blanks with your own example.)

- Brainstorm a list of words, ideas, sentences, or ways one might use an object. _____
  _____
  _____
  _____

- Invent a new title, ending, plot sequence, or character. _____
  _____
  _____
  _____

- Invent a new simile, metaphor, idiom, or other figure of speech.
  _____
  _____
  _____
  _____

- Imagine what might happen if the plot, a grammatical rule, or conventional spelling were changed. _____
  _____
  _____
  _____

- Create a dictionary, puzzle, story problem, or game. _____

_____

_____

_____

The study of poetry lends itself particularly well to creative thinking. Poetry can easily be incorporated into almost any unit. Vocabulary, for example, can be taught through poetry, which often illustrates nuances of meaning. In addition to reading poetry, students enjoy creating poems to show what they have learned. Your students may like to create a "biography poem" in which they write a line of free verse for each important life fact they learn while reading someone's biography.

Tables 9 and 10 present further examples of creative activities.

Table 9 Creative Activity From an Elementary School Lesson on the Genre of Tales (Specifically on "Wonder Tales" about animals' origins)

Rhyming Brainstorm Activity

Teacher Instructions:

Ask the children if they can generate other words that rhyme with "sleep" as you list students' ideas on chart paper. Then ask the children to review the list and brainstorm other "wonderful" reasons why bears sleep and what they might be dreaming about. For example, they might say bears sleep because they fell in a heap or that they are dreaming of a ride in a jeep. List students' ideas on chart paper. Encourage fluency and originality (see Teacher's Toolbox below). If students are unfamiliar with brainstorming, teachers should teach and model brainstorming before doing the Rhyming Brainstorm activity.

Teacher's Tool Box

Brainstorming

Brainstorming is a **creative** thinking activity in which students generate **many ideas** (fluency), **different ideas** (flexibility), **unusual ideas** (originality), and/or **interesting ideas** (elaboration).

To encourage **fluency**: encourage quantity not quality (defer judgment); push for more ideas (e.g., add to the list); keep it going (no conversations).

To encourage **originality**: think up all the usual ideas first (a "brain drain"); try to add ideas no one else might think of.

Table 10	Creative Language Arts Activity From a High School Lesson on the Literary Movement of Romanticism

Individual Activity (written assignment to hand in):

Suppose that Ralph Waldo Emerson was coming to your school and that you could meet with him. Imagine what would happen, what you might say to him or what you might ask about, and how he would react.

SCIENCE

Whatever our content area, we typically have *one* activity that we think of as *the* creative activity. Language arts teachers often use creative writing as a creative learning experience. For a science teacher, the first creative activity that comes to mind might be to design an experiment. How about using creative writing to reinforce science concepts for a change? For example, in an elementary school lesson on light that we designed, one of the suggested student activities is to write a conversation that might take place between a person who wears convex lenses and a person who wears concave lenses in a game situation. Convex lenses function as a magnifying glass, so the person wearing them will see surrounding objects as much bigger than they really are, while the person wearing concave lenses will have the opposite experience. Convex lenses are used for people with farsightedness (one form of which is also known as presbyopia, when the eye sees objects in the distance as normal, but objects that are close appear blurred), whereas concave lenses are used for people with nearsightedness (also known as myopia, when the eye sees near objects within a certain range very clearly while distant objects appear blurry at all times). Another example of a creative activity in science is for students to design a mirror maze as a culminating activity after having studied mirrors.

Even activities that are typically thought of as analytical, such as representing information graphically, can be given creative license. You might encourage your students to create a cartoon strip to illustrate the key concepts of a lesson or the main results of an experiment. Asking students to brainstorm unusual ways to prove a scientific concept provides them with another creative learning experience.

The following are some typical creative tasks in science that can be applied to a variety of curriculum topics. (Feel free to fill in the blanks with your own examples.)

- Explore ways light can be separated into different colors using different objects and how the process could be reversed. _____

  _____

  _____

  _____

- Create a cartoon strip illustrating the key concepts learned in this unit; or create new transparent and translucent objects by combining as many materials as possible. _____

  _____

  _____

  _____

- Brainstorm a list of words, ideas, or ways one might use a given object. _____

  _____

  _____

  _____

- Imagine what might happen if plants grew only in the dark or if your image in the mirror had a life of its own. _____

  _____

  _____

  _____

Tables 11 and 12 give further examples of creative student activities.

MATHEMATICS

When we ask mathematics teachers to think of creative learning experiences, we are often told that they cannot imagine how mathematical thinking, at the K–12 level, can be creative in nature. However, there are effective ways to infuse activities into mathematics learning experiences to develop students' creative thinking. For example, when students create their own number patterns or tessellations[1], they use creative thinking. Even concepts that are typically taught through analytical activities can be enhanced with creative activities. For example, you can help your students understand the concepts of two- and three-dimensional space by having them imagine they woke up one day as a two-dimensional person. Students can invent riddles that describe the properties of a shape and give them to their peers to solve. This activity allows

Table 11 Creative Activity From an Elementary School Science Lesson on Sound

This activity is taken from a curriculum in which students use LEGO and the engineering design process to learn about the science concept of sound. Review with students the instructions for building their maracas (musical instrument).

Student Instructions:

1. Choose small LEGO pieces to act as their maraca's noisemakers (e.g., connector pegs, short axles, 1x2 bricks, bushings).

2. Build a box or other hollow container that will hold the small noisemaker pieces.

3. Put the noisemakers inside the container.

4. Build a cover or lid for the container.

5. Shake the container and listen to the maraca's noise.

Sample LEGO maracas.

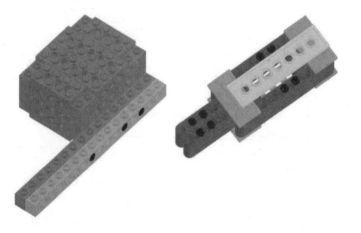

- Explain that if students finish building their maracas before others, they should draw and label a diagram of it in their notebook.

Table 12 Creative Activity From a High School Lesson on Vectors

---

Graphical Addition of Vectors

Student Instructions:

1. Create a vector game or puzzle for your classmates to solve. It could be a board game, a maze, a riddle, a mystery, a treasure hunt, or anything else that you wish. It should use three-dimensional vectors. Trade games/puzzles with one of your classmates and see if he or she solves it correctly.

Teacher Instructions:

These questions and activities may be completed in class or assigned as homework. The vector game or puzzle can either be done independently or in small groups. If each student designs a vector puzzle, it can be short (three–five vectors). Make sure that students record the solution for the vector puzzles they design so their classmates can check their results. If the vector puzzles are created in small groups, you may want to require a puzzle using up to ten vectors. Puzzles can be swapped among groups. Encourage creativity in this activity. Students may choose to make up a game, puzzle, riddle, mystery, treasure hunt, or anything else.

---

them to be creative in developing the riddles, while also understanding the distinct combination of properties that characterize each geometric figure.

In one mathematics unit targeting measurement skills that we developed for elementary schools, students were asked to create a system of measurement to develop their understanding of the importance of standard versus nonstandard systems of measurement and how different standard systems have emerged (metric and customary). In addition, you might encourage your students to use creative activities as a study or memory strategy for rote mathematical processes, such as long division procedures or times tables. For example, in a unit we developed targeting equivalent fractions, described in Table 13, students were given creative drawings of the 1/2 fraction family and asked to draw their own fraction family to help automatically encode some of the most commonly found equivalent fractions.

Most data collection and representation projects culminate in a presentation of the data. Asking students to brainstorm unusual ways to demonstrate what they have found provides yet another creative learning experience, such as in our example in Table 13.

Table 13 Creative Activity From a Mathematics Unit on Equivalent Fractions

Student Instructions:

Imagine that all of the fractions equivalent to $\frac{1}{2}$ are a family. In the space below or on another piece of paper, draw what you imagine the members of this family would look like. Remember, my family looked like this. They all have a circle stomach that shows what fraction they are.

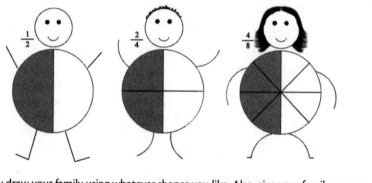

You may draw your family using whatever shapes you like. Also, give your family a name.

The following are some typical creative mathematics tasks that can be applied to a variety of curriculum topics:

- Imagine something unexpected has happened; for example, you have shrunk to 1/3 your size, your classroom has become spherical in shape, or positive numbers have become negative. _____
- Invent a new system of numbers, or system of measurement. _____
- Come up with a question to ask for a data collection, or a strategy for remembering a procedure or fact. _____

Tables 14 and 15 provide further examples of creative activities in math.

Table 14 Creative Activity From an Elementary School Math Lesson on Data Analysis and Representation

Teacher Instructions:

1. Discuss and review the previous homework assignment. Ensure that students have a good understanding of bar graphs and answer any questions they may have.

2. Introduce the concept that there are different types of graphs and that today students will be learning about pictographs. Refer to a survey that you will have had students conduct in class (for example, of students' favorite ice cream flavors) and demonstrate how the results of this survey could also be shown in a pictograph, such as in the example below.

Example Pictograph:

☺ = 2 people (half a face represents one person)

Chocolate	☺☺☺
Strawberry	☺☺☺
Vanilla	☺
Chocolate Chip	☺☺☺☺

Explain that pictographs use pictures to represent numbers and that the faces (or whatever picture you use) represent how many people chose the ice cream flavor as their favorite. Show how, in pictographs, one picture can stand for two or more people or things. Ask the students to think of something besides faces (or the picture you use) that you could have used to represent the results of this study.

3. Now have students help you create a second example of a pictograph. You may want to use an example from your class, for example, the color of the students' hair or shirts or types of shoes they are wearing. Demonstrate again how a picture could represent more than one object or person. If you think students need more practice, have them help you create a third pictograph.

Table 15   Creative Activity From a Middle School Lesson on Numbers

---

Characters in a TV Show

Student Instructions:

Imagine that "Million," "Billion," "Trillion," "Quadrillion," and "Quintillion" are the characters of a new TV show. List two or three adjectives to describe what each one of them looks like, and describe how they are related to one another. If you want to, you can make a drawing of each character.

Teacher Instructions:

Go through the answers orally in class.
Million:

Billion:

Trillion:

Quadrillion:

Quintillion:

How are Million, Billion, Trillion, Quadrillion, and Quintillion related?

SOCIAL SCIENCES

One creative activity that is suitable to history and world culture classes is to ask students to put themselves in someone else's shoes and to imagine what life was like at a different historical period, or what life is like in a different geographical and cultural context. For example, as a culminating activity to an upper middle school curriculum on slavery in the United States, we asked that students engage in an activity we called "Just like you." Students were asked to draw a painting of a teenager who lived in the seventeenth or eighteenth century and who is being transported to the United States as either an indentured servant or a slave. They were asked to refer back to their text- and workbooks to make the drawing historically accurate, and to prepare a short story or a biography of the person to be presented to the rest of the class along with the painting. Students were given the following guiding questions, but are otherwise free to let their imagination flow. Think of the following questions:

> What is the name of your character? Where does he or she come from? Who are his/her parents? Why is your character on the ship? What are the conditions on the ship that your character has to endure? Where does he/she sleep? What does he/she eat? What will happen to your character once the ship reaches the United States?

Tables 16 and 17 provide further examples of creative activities in the social sciences.

Table 16   Creative Activity From a High School Lesson on Psychology

Name:

Worksheet: Physical Changes During Adolescence

We have seen in today's reading that the biological changes during adolescence can start at different ages, depending on each individual. This difference between one's own growth rate and that of classmates and friends can sometimes be a problem, both for those who develop earlier than most and for those who develop more slowly.

Imagine what it would be like if everybody developed at exactly the same moment and at the same speed.

Suppose that this was the case in your school. List two positive things and two negative things about this situation.

Positive   **Negative**

Table 17   Creative Activity From a High School Lesson on World Cultures

---

Name:

Worksheet: Mexican Culture Before the Spanish Invasion

When the Spanish conquered Mexico, the dominant culture was the Aztec culture. Mythological animals played an important part in the Aztec culture, and archeologists have found many engravings and sculptures representing these magical animals. On the enclosed drawing, you will see some representations of the dog Itzcuintli.

Based on these drawings, imagine what Itzcuintli stands for. What kind of powers do you think Itzcuintli has? Is Itzcuintli a good or an evil force?

List a few characteristics below and share your image of Itzcuintli with the rest of the class.

_____

_____

_____

_____

_____

CLOSING ACTIVITY

Now try to come up with a creative activity in which you could engage your students. Don't worry too much for now about the potential logistical difficulties associated with implementing this activity in the classroom. The goal is to stretch your imagination and think of how you could be more creative, and to allow your students to build their creative strengths in the subject you teach. So be creative!

Content Area:

_____

_____

_____

_____

Activity:

_____

_____

_____

_____

_____

How to Enhance Practical Skills

What teacher has never heard a student ask, "Why do we have to learn this?" Sometimes the question is just there to mark frustration, but more often than not, it's a legitimate question. When you plan your curriculum, you should keep it in the back of your mind, for certainly there is a goal (implicit or explicit) for anything we teach. Sometimes the reason we teach a given concept is to provide students with a stepping stone so that they will understand what comes next, but in most cases we should also be able to think of reasons why students would need the knowledge we teach them in living their own life. You can also use biographies or movies to show students examples of people who use the concepts you teach in their professional lives. This ability to apply knowledge to real-world situations is an illustration of practical skills. By demonstrating your own practical strengths in showing students how to relate classroom knowledge to real-world application, you will help students strengthen their practical skills. You will also capture the attention of those students who, without wanting to raise the question out loud, wonder why they have to learn something. In this chapter we will provide examples of how you can enhance students' practical skills in a number of content areas.

LANGUAGE ARTS

Language arts teachers continually encourage students to describe their initial reactions to literature and to make text-to-self connections. Effective language arts instruction includes teaching students to interact with the text as they read, ask questions, note similarities between what they read and what they experience in their own lives, and interpret the author's theme or message. Teaching for practical intelligence can provide students with opportunities to explore literature from a personal perspective. In fact, as language arts teachers, we most likely intuitively draw on practical activities to encourage children to make personal connections to the text. If we combine such practical activities with explicit instruction in practical intelligence, we promote students' metacognition. When students are aware of their own thinking, they are more likely to call on those cognitive processes when they read independently outside the classroom. After all, in "real life," readers are not prompted by a teacher's set of comprehension questions but are left to question, interpret, and construct meaning from text in ways that are personally relevant. In sum, practical learning experiences encourage students to apply their knowledge in authentic contexts.

The following language arts skills are essentially practical in nature. (Please fill in the blanks with your own example.)

- Apply what you have just learned about the past tense to rewrite the story as if it took place in the past, or use your new vocabulary to add details to a description. _____

  _____

  _____

  _____

- Connect the lessons learned from a character in a novel to real life.

  _____

  _____

  _____

- Find examples in real life that mirror those described in the story.

  _____

  _____

  _____

  _____

- Translate the fictional ending to how the story would most likely end in real life. _____

  _____

  _____

Tables 18 and 19 provide further examples of language arts concepts that lend themselves to instruction in the practical mode.

Table 18 Elementary School Language Arts Concepts That Lend Themselves to Instruction in the Practical Mode

Language Arts Concept	Practical Instruction
Text-to-self connections Relating to characters Learning lessons (inference) Drawing upon prior knowledge to interpret text	Teach students to ask themselves questions, such as "Does this character remind me of someone I know?" "What might I do if I were in [character's] situation?"
Writing Skills Biographical/autobiographical sketches Authentic writing tasks	Design writing tasks that students would use in real-life situations, such as letters to editors or pen pals, or persuasive letters convincing "real" audiences, such as congresspersons or consumer advocates.

Table 19 Practical Activity From a Lesson Accompanying the Reading of Harper Lee's *To Kill a Mocking Bird*

Student Instructions (divided in small groups):

As in the previous chapter, Miss Caroline seems to have trouble with her Maycomb class. She does not know or understand many of the things that Maycomb children take for granted, for example that Walter Cunningham does not have enough money for lunch, or that Burris Ewell comes from a family where you don't wash and don't go to school. This is something the children know without anyone ever explicitly telling them. Show how the same is true in your school. What things do you know and take for granted that would be difficult for a new teacher to understand? You can also apply the situation to the schoolyard: what does a new student in school have to learn without anyone explicitly telling him or her in order to be accepted? Try to think of all the *dos* and *don'ts* and list them.

_____

_____

_____

_____

SCIENCE

Teaching for practical intelligence provides students opportunities to understand how science has an impact on their daily lives. For example, if you know something about how plants grow, you can grow them at home. If you know that water freezes at 32° Fahrenheit, you can predict that the water you left outside for your pet rabbit will freeze at that temperature and your pet will not be able to drink. Most science teachers intuitively draw on practical activities to encourage children to make personal connections to the concepts that are taught. If we combine such practical activities with explicit instruction in practical intelligence, we promote students' metacognition, as explained in the language arts section above. When students are aware of their own thinking, they are more likely to call on those cognitive processes outside the classroom.

For example, in a series of elementary school science lessons on magnets, students used their practical intelligence and understanding of magnets to design a test to guard against magnetic interference with a compass. Students were divided into pairs and given the following instructions:

> You are going on a camping trip. You want to take five different magnets with you as well as a compass. From the last lesson, you know that a magnet can upset a compass. You only have a small bag to carry all your stuff. Design a test (not using the compass) to make sure that your magnets do not interfere with your compass. Use the space provided to explain your test.

After the students designed a test, the teacher recorded each pair's answer. Possible student solutions included wrapping a magnet in materials and testing for magnetism by holding another magnet on the outside of the wrapped magnet. If the wrapped magnet was not strong enough to attract the outside magnet, then it would not affect the needle of a compass.

The following science skills are essentially practical in nature. (Please fill in the blanks with your own example.)

- Apply the safety precautions you have read about to your behavior in the lab, or the instructions on how to use the microscope to study a slide. _____
  _____
  _____
  _____

- Implement the experimental protocol that you have designed, or the suggested changes to your three-dimensional model.

  _____

  _____

  _____

  _____

- Find examples in your life when you used your knowledge of biology.

  _____

  _____

  _____

  _____

- Demonstrate your understanding of physics by building a simple water purifier. _____

  _____

  _____

  _____

Tables 20 and 21 provide further examples of practical science activities.

Table 20 Practical Activity From an Elementary School Lesson on Ecology

This activity follows a lesson in which students engage in the analytical activity of planning a terrarium garden.

Student Instructions:

Place your soil into the terrarium. Using your grid pattern as a guide, use a toothpick to mark the space allocated for each type of plant.

Use the toothpicks with the color dots to mark the area where you want to plant the seeds. Use as many toothpicks and color dots as you need.

Take turns planting your seeds. Make sure that the place each seed is planted matches the place on your grid-map. Take turns with your partner in planting seeds and checking the grid map.

Table 21 Practical Activity From a High School Physics Lesson on Vectors and Scalars

---

Teacher Instructions:

After showing students how to find distance and direction and how to draw vectors using airplane data and maps, ask students to identify other real world examples of vectors and scalars.

MATHEMATICS

Mathematics teachers increasingly encourage students to make practical connections between mathematics concepts and events, objects, and concepts in the student's world. Making connections to their own lives encourages students to see the utility of the sometimes abstract concepts found in mathematics. Effective mathematics instruction includes teaching students to ask questions and to note similarities between what they learn and what they experience in their own lives. Teaching for practical intelligence can provide students opportunities to explore mathematics from a personal perspective. By increasing their connections to the content they learn, we increase students' ability to remember the concepts. As we have noted, mathematics textbooks have increasingly included practical connections.

For example, in a curriculum unit on number sense that we created, students used their practical intelligence to give directions on a map using the concepts of parallel and intersecting lines (roads). They also read a thermometer to understand the number line, including positive and negative numbers, and used $1, $10, and $100 bills to understand the concept of place value. Students discussed the role of numbers in their world, solved practical number problems, and found five interesting facts on a number of their choice. They were told:

> Did you know that 18 equilateral triangles make a hexagon ring? Or that Australian football is played with teams of 18 players? How much do you know about a number? Choose one number and see what you can find out! Write your number in the space below and then write everything you find. Find and record at least five facts about your number.

Thus, students learned about numbers through learning experiences related to their own lives. In sum, practical learning encourages students to apply their knowledge in authentic contexts.

The following mathematics skills are essentially practical in nature. (Please fill in the blanks with your own example.)

- Apply a mathematical rule to solving equations. _____
  _____
  _____
  _____

- Use mathematical notation to show the relationship between two data points. _____
  _____
  _____
  _____

- Find examples in real life when you need to calculate a diameter.
  _____
  _____
  _____
  _____

- Demonstrate how entity A relates to entity B. _____
  _____
  _____
  _____

Tables 22 and 23 provide further examples.

Table 22 Practical Activity From an Elementary School Lesson on Measurement

Increasing Recipes

Materials:

- recipes
- recipe ingredients

Teacher Instructions:

1. Divide the students into small groups.
2. Give each group a different recipe (make sure that they are recipes for things that don't have to be cooked or baked, such as trail mix) and have each group double or triple the recipe to make enough for everyone in the classroom.
3. Have each group explain how they increased the recipe so that it was enough for the entire class.

Table 23 Practical Activity From a High School Lesson on Prime and Composite Numbers

---

Name:

Worksheet: Think of Prime Numbers and Composite Numbers

Think of the different objects in your classroom and at home. Some things exist in large quantities (chairs in a classroom), some in lesser quantities (rooms in your home). Now think of three prime numbers and three composite numbers, and find an illustration for each one of them among the objects in your classroom or home. For example, you can think of the composite number 30 illustrated by the number of chairs in your classroom, and the prime number 3 illustrated by the number of rooms in your house.

Prime Numbers

First Prime Number: _____
Object:

Second Prime Number: _____
Object:

Third Prime Number: _____
Object:

Composite Numbers

First Composite Number: _____
Object:

Second Composite Number: _____
Object:

Third Composite Number: _____
Object:

SOCIAL SCIENCES

One practical activity that is easily applicable to the social sciences is to ask students to apply a historical or cultural lesson to their own lives. For example, in a history lesson on the prejudice European settlers in the New World felt against indigenous populations, students are encouraged to consider that prejudice still exists today. They are further urged to think of two examples, one when they were the recipient and one when they were the perpetrator of prejudice.

One way to start the classroom discussion is to ask students to think of what comes to their minds when they see homeless people on the corner begging for loose change from passersby. Do they think that the homeless must be on drugs, or were fired from their jobs because they could not keep up with the workload? Or do they balance those thoughts with the notion that these people could possibly have a mental illness or have been forced to leave home at a very young age? Students are thus encouraged to apply the historical lesson to their daily life and to see the connection between past and present.

Tables 24 and 25 provide further examples of practical activities in the social sciences.

Table 24 Practical Activity From a High School Lesson on Psychology (and the concept of adolescence, in particular)

Activity (30 minutes):

Hand out the enclosed poll-sheets and ask students to divide them in half: one for boys and one for girls. The goal is to make a rapid poll in the classroom on qualities rated most important in the opposite sex.

On each sheet, there is a list of nine attributes. Ask students to rank these attributes, with 1 the most important and 9 the least important.

Write down the two lists of attributes on the board. Go through the answers for boys, then the answers for girls. Count the number of times each attribute was ranked as number one. Repeat for all attributes and for both boys and girls.

How important are the following attributes for a boy? Rank them from 1 (the most important) to 9 (the least important).	How important are the following attributes for a girl? Rank them from 1 (the most important) to 9 (the least important).
intelligence	intelligence
attractiveness	attractiveness
friendliness	friendliness
physical strength	physical strength
ability to hold a conversation	ability to hold a conversation
commitment	commitment
fitness	fitness
sense of humor	sense of humor
passion	passion

Table 25 Practical Activity From a Middle School Lesson on "The Birth of the Nation" (and the concept of historical maxims, in particular)

Maxims: Learning from the Past	
Estimated Time	35 minutes
Grouping	Pairs
Presentation Materials	None
Objectives	Students will practice their wise thinking by identifying wise sayings or maxims.
	Students will examine how these sayings can be used in real-life situations.
	Students will construct their own maxims and explain their applications.

Teacher Instructions:

a. Tell students that Franklin's ideas and his character can be seen not only through his actions and accomplishments, but also through his writings. One of his most popular works is *Poor Richard's Almanac*, an annual journal containing maxims and proverbs that provide advice for achieving success in the world.

b. Explain the word "maxim" to the students. Tell students that an ability to make good decisions often requires applying the knowledge learned from one's own past experiences or the experiences of others to the current situation. Sometimes people share what they have learned from their past experiences in the form of maxims. Explain how maxims are general rules for how to live. For instance, "They are sayings that give advice for different situations. They can be found in literature, in conversations with elders or friends, and sometimes even in fortune cookies."

c. Divide students into pairs and give them maxims from Franklin's *Poor Richard's Almanac* to interpret. Have students share their interpretations with the class. Point out to the students that through Franklin's maxims we can again trace Franklin's beliefs to the ideas of the Enlightenment. Take, for example, Franklin's maxim "God helps them that help themselves." Here, Franklin asserts his belief in the power of individuals to determine the course of their lives. In general, his maxims are concerned with how to live a productive, prosperous, and healthy life and are directed at matters that are secular, rather than spiritual. For Franklin, living a good life depends more on one's ability to exercise diligence and self-control than on God's sympathy.

d. Point out that, through maxims, people try to accumulate and share the valuable lessons learned from their life experience. Using past experience to make better decisions in the future is characteristic of *wise* people. Explain that, in this class, students will be developing their ability to make *wise* or sound judgments. Wisdom is a complex quality, and the class will be discussing its many different aspects during the next several weeks. For now, it is sufficient to say that sometimes people's collective wisdom is expressed in maxims. Maxims, or general rules about life, allow people to capture this accumulated wisdom and pass it from one generation to another.

e. Explain to students that the important thing to know about maxims is when or in what situations one should use them. Have students work in pairs to find examples for applying Franklin's maxims, coming up with their own maxims, and describing the situations where these maxims could be used.

f. Have several students share some of their own maxims and the applicable situations with the whole class. Reiterate to students that the ability to learn from the past, whether our own or that of other people, is an important skill. It allows one to resolve problems by making sounder and wiser judgments. It is always good to reflect on one's own experience and try to find a new general rule, or maxim, that can help one in a similar situation in the future. Suggest that students continue writing their own *wise sayings*, or maxims, in a notebook or a journal throughout the semester and the school year.

CLOSING ACTIVITY

Your turn again! Now think of a concept or lesson you teach that students typically perceive as dry or abstract. How could you help students see its relevance to their own lives and make it more practical? Remember to put yourself in your students' shoes. If you are much older than your students, for example, chances are that the people you think of as TV or movie stars are not the biggest stars in your students' worlds. If many of your students are first generation U.S. residents, what may seem to you as typical foods or sports may not appear as such to your students. Describe the activity and what real-life experience it relates to (and yes, this is a practical activity!).

Content Area:

_____

_____

_____

_____

Describe the activity and how it relates to "Real Life:"

_____

_____

_____

_____

Your Turn

Identify Different Types of Teaching Strategies

I n this part of the book, we have explained what teaching for memory, analytical, creative, and practical skills means. We have shown examples to illustrate how it can be done in real-world classrooms in a number of content areas and for different grade levels. Finally, we have encouraged you to come up with your own examples of analytical, creative, and practical teaching activities. As we stressed in the introductory part of this book, you are likely already using some of each type of activity in your classroom, so you should view this part of the book as a source of inspiration. Hopefully, you feel more assured, now that you have read this, that the different thinking skills can be enhanced in your classroom too. To help *all* students learn, irrespective of their preferred learning mode and strengths, what matters is to keep a *balance,* and to propose activities addressing analytical, creative, and practical skills (in addition to memory) in roughly equal measure. In the closing part of this book, we will return to this notion of balance and offer some curriculum-planning tools that can help you achieve it. First, though, we will review how we can assess for these different thinking skills, to ensure that teaching and assessment are aligned in our classrooms.

Before we move on to assessment, though, we propose a brief quiz to see what you have learned from this part of the book. In Table 26, you will find a list of activities that we ask you to classify as addressing mainly memory, analytical, practical, or creative skills. An Answer Key is provided at the end of the book.

Table 26 Culminating Quiz

Below you will find a description of six activities. Please classify these activities by indicating which cognitive skill they primarily address (choose among M for memory, A for analytical, C for creative, or P for practical).

Activity	Main skill (M, A, C, P)
[Psychology] Divide your students into small groups and ask each student to share with the group an example from their own life illustrating the concept of peer pressure.	
[Statistics] Share with students a set of statistical data on the effects of unhealthy food on health and ask them to imagine that they are working for an organic-fruit cooperative and must come up with an advertisement campaign to promote their product, using the data in a creative way.	
[Geography] Give your students a list of all the countries in the European Union and ask them to compare and contrast them, categorizing them by the initial letter of their name.	
[Literature] Ask students to analyze how the author uses language to indicate that some text passages refer to the narrator's past and others to the present.	
[Physical Education] Assign a pair of students to each track & field activity in which you will engage them (long jump, triple jump, broad jump, pole vault, javelin, discus, etc.) and ask them to learn the rules so that their peers can ask them about it as needed.	
[Biology] Divide your students into small teams and assign each team the role of a marine creature living in coral reefs. Ask them to look up information about "their" animal (habitat, eating, and reproductive habits, etc.) and then have them role-play a discussion in which each creature argues for its right to resources in an ocean where coral reefs are disappearing.	

NOTE

1. Tessellations are repetitions of shapes, such as are often seen in floor tiling or mosaics, where a given geometrical shape is repeated again and again.

PART III

Integrating Teaching and Assessment in Your Classroom

Introduction to Integrating Teaching and Assessment

In Part III, we will start by reminding you of the necessity to match teaching and assessment practices, and then we will provide empirical reasons for broadening testing practices to assess creative and practical abilities in addition to memory and analytical skills. We will not cite any research findings in this part, but if you are interested in finding out more about our research and how we have tested the benefits of assessing for a broader array of skills, you can consult the Appendix to Part I at the end of this book. Finally, we will describe how we develop analytical, creative, and practical assessment items, both in a multiple-choice and open-ended format, and present sample assessment items in different content areas. We will also describe the rubrics we developed to rate student responses to the open-response items. In the Appendix to Part III, you will find a table cross-referencing the examples by content area and grade level. We will also encourage you to come up with your own examples, and we will end with a brief quiz to see how savvy you have become at identifying assessment items tapping into different thinking skills!

11

Matching Assessment and Instruction

One major goal of instruction is the creation of expertise through a well organized, easily retrievable knowledge base. Assessment must match instruction—you must assess what you teach and teach what you will assess. If you address a broad range of strengths when you teach, you should address an equally broad range of skills when you assess your students. Many teachers incorporate creative and practical activities in their teaching, but may feel at loss when it comes to assessing creativity, practical skills, or wise thinking. As a result, they may end up assessing students only for their memory and analytical skills.

Narrow assessment is problematic for several reasons. First, if there is a lack of balance between what is taught and what is assessed, students will quickly feel that some classroom activities (i.e., the creative and practical ones) are not as important as are others (i.e., the analytical and memory ones), because they never appear on the test. Students will not feel encouraged to take all activities as seriously. Second, if you assess only a narrow range of skills, few students will be able to capitalize on their strengths to learn better and to experience a rewarding feeling of success in the classroom. All skills count, and we are not promoting the idea that some students are "just creative" and should not be taught and assessed for memory or analytical skills. But we do believe that the "creative student" will benefit from a teaching style that addresses several skills and be able to capitalize on the areas of strength to work on the areas of weakness.

Similarly, by being assessed in a domain of strength (such as for creative skills), the student will be able to display strengths and have a more positive experience than if she or he were assessed in an area of weakness alone. Analytical, creative, and practical skills are all important for success in life (whether in school, in one's personal life, and on the job). So let's assess for all skills and give all students a chance to shine. Indeed, our research shows that students who may be mediocre or even poor students when taught conventionally can perform much better when taught for successful intelligence.

General Guidelines for Developing Diversified Assessments

I n this chapter, we will discuss the development of multiple-choice and open-ended assessments that address a range of cognitive skills. That is not to say that these are the only two forms of assessment, but they are the most commonly used in schools. Authentic, performance-based assessment is another very valuable form of assessment, but we will not discuss it here.

We typically use a three-step approach to developing multiple-choice and open-ended items to assess for memory, analytical, creative, and practical skills. As you read along, we encourage you to focus on one topic that you teach, and to develop examples of your own. We've provided tables for you to complete, but you can also keep a pad of paper or your laptop handy as you read and jot down your ideas there.

Step 1

When developing assessments, the first task is to determine what the most important concepts and skills are with which students should walk away. When we develop curriculum units or lesson plans, we always start by listing all the standards, key concepts, and skills addressed, as illustrated in Table 27. You can use Table 28 to develop your own lesson overview.

Table 27 Determining the Most Important Concepts and Skills Addressed in a Curriculum Unit: An Illustration From a Fourth Grade Science Unit on Light

The Nature of Light

Purpose

The purpose of this unit is to provide students with a basic understanding of the properties of light. In addition, students will develop the skills necessary to conduct scientific investigations and gain an appreciation for science as a discipline. (Note: This unit is consistent with the applicable standards for science for grades K–4 in the districts in which we worked. Here we present the standards that applied in the districts we developed this curriculum for, as an illustration. Find out what standards apply in your district!)

Overview of Objectives

Content-Based Objectives

By the end of this unit, students will be able to:

- show that light travels in straight lines (*lesson 1*)
- define *transparent, translucent,* and *opaque* and give examples of each (*lesson 1*)
- explain how mirrors reflect light (*lesson 2*)
- describe and give examples of refraction (*lesson 3*)
- explain the relationship between lenses and refraction (*lesson 4*)
- explain the differences between *convex* and *concave* (*lesson 4*)
- give examples illustrating that visible light is made up of different colors (*lesson 5*)
- list colors that compose visible light (*lesson 5*)
- give examples of absorption (*lesson 6*)
- describe the similarities and differences between absorption and reflection (*lesson 6*)

Performance-Based Objectives

By the end of this unit, students will be able to:

- demonstrate the differences between transparent, translucent, and opaque objects (*lesson 1*)
- use observations to support conclusions about a phenomenon (*lessons 1–6*)
- illustrate that images in mirrors are reversed (*lesson 2*)
- make predictions and use observational data to support their predictions (*lessons 1–6*)

- illustrate that the angle of incidence is equal to the angle of reflection *(lesson 3)*
- create a collage that shows how lenses are used in everyday life *(lesson 4)*
- set up a demonstration that shows the differences between concave and convex lenses *(lesson 4)*
- show that visible light is composed of different colors *(lesson 5)*

Content Standards

- Light travels in straight lines until it strikes an object.
- Light can be reflected by a mirror, refracted by a lens, or absorbed by an object.

Process Standards

Students should be able to:

- ask questions about objects and events in the environment
- plan and conduct a simple investigation
- employ simple equipment and tools to gather data and extend the senses
- use data to construct a reasonable explanation
- communicate the results of investigations and explanations

Unifying Concepts and Processes

- evidence, models, and explanations
- change, constancy, and measurement

Table 28   Step 1: Develop Your Own Lesson Plan

Content area: _____

Lesson topic: _____

Objectives for this lesson: (You can also modify this table to cover a sequence of lessons [a unit] rather than a single lesson.)

   Content. By the end of this lesson, students will be able to:

- _____
- _____
- _____
- _____

(Continued)

(Continued)

Skills. By the end of this lesson, students will be able to:

- _____
- _____
- _____
- _____

This lesson addresses the following standards as outlined by the district/the state/the content area's national association (as applicable):

- _____
- _____
- _____
- _____

I will assess if my students have met the learning goals by:

- _____
- _____
- _____
- _____

Step 2

The second task is to determine how many, and which, levels of ability should be assessed for each cognitive skill (memory, analytical, creative, and practical). Most classrooms group together students by different levels of ability. It is therefore important to address a range of abilities in the assessment, so that all students will be able to answer at least some of the questions. We often use a 5-point proficiency (or competency) scale, but you can choose a more narrow (e.g., 3-point) or broader (e.g., 7-point) scale, depending on the complexity of the content you teach (or plan to teach) and the range of abilities in your classroom. If your students are homogeneous in terms of abilities, it might be hard to distinguish them on a 7-point scale, and you might prefer a 3-point scale. On the other hand, if you teach in an inclusive classroom where students' abilities vary greatly, a 7-point scale will enable you to develop assessment items targeted both for the lower achieving and the very highly achieving students.

In other cases, you want to assess students' threshold mastery, in other words, whether students have achieved a certain competency or acquired a piece of knowledge. In those cases, you will not use a scale of items of varying levels of difficulty, but rather, code students' answers as 0 (incorrect) or 1 (correct). For example, suppose you want to determine whether all students in your class can add single-digit numbers before you move on to teaching the addition of double-digit numbers; you then can give them three–five arithmetic problems to solve (e.g., $2 + 2 = ?$, $2 + 3 = ?$, $5 + 4 = ?$) and rate the responses as 0 or 1.

Table 29 provides a 5-point ability scale for assessment items targeting memory skills that we developed for use in elementary schools. This scale illustrates what an "easy" (1-point) item should assess, what a slightly higher level 2-point item should assess, and so forth. You will find additional examples further on, under the corresponding skill (analytical, creative, practical) heading.

Think of how Step 2 would apply in your own classroom—or imagine how it will apply in your future class. Take a topic or concept that you recently taught (or that of the lesson plan you outlined in Table 28), and come up with three questions of varying difficulty level focusing on that one topic. You can write down your answers in Table 30.

Table 29   A 5-Point Proficiency Scale for Items Assessing Memory Skills in Mathematics

Level 1. The task requires recognition of one term, vocabulary word, or its definition. The terms and definitions have been explicitly taught and applied throughout the unit (e.g., recognizing a line with an arrow at one end as "a ray," given a list of choices).

Level 2. The task requires cued recall of one term, vocabulary word, or its definition (e.g., identifying a "right angle" from among a set of angles).

Level 3. The task requires active recall of concepts, terms, vocabulary words, or their definitions (e.g., drawing an example of lines that "intersect").

Level 4. The task requires active recall of a list or the identification of missing pieces of information in a sequenced or nonsequenced list (e.g., describing the sequence of tasks when conducting data collection and analysis).

Level 5. The task requires production of paraphrase, summary, or synonym; and requires application of skills (e.g., describing what you are measuring when you measure the "volume" of something).

Table 30   Develop Your Own Assessment Questions

This exercise will be even more helpful if you have a colleague to pair up with so that you can discuss your ideas and make sure that you agree on the difficulty levels. If you're working with a colleague, you may want to draft the three questions and then give them to your colleague and ask them to classify the questions by order of difficulty, to see if you agree.

Concept or skill to be assessed: _____

_____

_____

(A)   An easy item to assess this concept or skill:

_____

_____

(B)   An intermediate level item to assess this concept or skill:

_____

_____

Why is B harder than A?

_____

_____

(C)   A high-level item to assess this concept or skill:

_____

_____

Why is C harder than B?

_____

_____

Step 3

The third step in diversified assessments is to write the actual items and ensure a balance between (1) memory, analytical, creative, and practical skills, and (2) multiple-choice and open-ended item formats. All item formats present their specific challenges and advantages, and we recommend that you use a range of item formats, in the same manner that you address a range of thinking skills. Here, we review two major forms of written assessment, but performance-based assessment in authentic settings is another type of assessment you might want to consider. The closed answer format (e.g., multiple-choice, true/false, matching) presents the advantage of being quick and easy to score in a reliable fashion. (Sometimes you can even have a machine do the job for you.)

This format, however, is not as beneficial as open-ended items in assessing higher order thinking skills, including creativity. At the same time, open-ended items (e.g., short answer, essay, oral presentation) require that you develop a rubric for scoring answers, and typically take more time to score than do closed format items. To help you develop items in different formats, the rest of Part III will focus on Step 3. We will provide plenty of examples of assessment items in closed and open-ended answer formats, in different content areas, and for different grade levels.

Assessing and Rating Memory Skills

Memory items require students to recall and/or recognize who did certain things (e.g., who was the hero in the story), what things they did (e.g., what Martin Luther King's contributions to the Civil Rights movement were), how certain things are done (e.g., how two fractions are added), or when certain things are done (e.g., when plants reject carbon dioxide).

Let's look at examples in different content areas.

LANGUAGE ARTS

The following example of an open-ended response item designed to assess memory skills is pulled from an elementary school language arts unit called "True Wonders." In the end-of-unit assessment, students are given a brief paragraph to read about beavers, and then are asked to "Write in your own words something you learned in this article." Accurate answers should restate something the student has read, but the number of points attributed to the answer will vary on a 0 to 5 point scale, depending on the level of accuracy and complexity of the answer. In Table 31, we indicate what elements are necessary for an answer to be given—0, 1, 2, 3, 4, or 5 points respectively—and show sample responses that received these different scores.

Table 31 Rubric for Attributing a Score to a Language Arts Memory Assessment Item From an Elementary School Lesson on the "Wonder Tales" Genre

Value	Description of Value	Examples of Responses
0	Completely wrong or off-topic.	*Well, I saw someone who . . .*
1	Minimal attempt to answer the question; little or no recognition of the target content; incorrect answer; "wild guess" that is somewhat related to the question.	*How do they build their home* (minimal attempt; no recognition). Anything repeated word for word.
2	Incorrect answer but some recognition of the content; the answer is clearly related to the question; answer may repeat words or cues in the question.	*Beavers are known for building things* (repeats word for word from the passage); *beavers eat wood* (incorrect—beavers chew through wood; they do not eat it). Anything repeated word for word.
3	A partially correct, vague, or non-specific answer; some active recall.	*That beavers are related to the rodent family and beavers live throughout North America* ("related" to the rodent family is not the same as being a member of the rodent family). A statement that is in their own words, but got a fact confused, or is vague or partially correct.
4	Answer demonstrates a basic understanding of the new material; active recall; correct answer; answer is not elaborated and may appear "formulaic" or a "textbook" definition.	*Beavers build houses and live in the water* (correct). Can be simple, as long as it is in their own words, and correct.
5	A correct answer that includes elaboration, paraphrase, or summary; the answer may demonstrate transfer of learning.	*Beavers are known for building things. I knew that they chew wood, but I didn't know that they were "known for building things"* (goes beyond the question to connect/compare with prior knowledge). Really unusual answers.

SCIENCE

As we saw in Part II, you can infuse any content area with memory, analytical, creative, and practical thinking skills, and the same goes for assessment. In other words, you can assess primarily for memory skills in science as well as in physics, second languages, or the arts. Here is an example of a multiple-choice question, taken from an elementary school science lesson on light, tapping primarily memory skills. Students are asked, "Which of the following objects will let the most light pass through it?" and then are asked to circle one of four response options: (a) solid object, (b) translucent object, (c) transparent object, or (d) opaque object.

This is a memory item because unless you remember what the terms *translucent, transparent* and *opaque* mean, you will not be able correctly to answer the question.

Next is an example of an open-ended response item in science designed to assess memory skills. It is pulled from a high school Advanced Placement (A.P.)[1] level physics assessment, which our group developed. In Table 32, we provide the item and the scoring rubric.

Table 32 High School Physics Item Primarily Assessing Memory Skills

Task:

You are a member of the first group from Earth to land on the surface of Europa, a satellite of Jupiter. It is known from accurate telescopic observations that Europa is a sphere of radius 1570 km; it has no atmosphere.

Inside the spacecraft you place a 0.500 kg mass on an electronic balance. It weighs 0.66 Newtons [N].

How great is the acceleration of gravity on Europa?

Rubric:

For each step, the student receives 1 point for a correct formula (max 2 points) and 1 point for a correct calculation (max 2 points), plus a point for a correct final answer. The possible total score for this question thus ranges from 0–5 points.

(i)

Formula: $W = mg$

Calculation: $0.66 = 0.5g$, so $g = 1.32 = 1.3$ m/s^2

(ii)

Formula: $F = GMm/r^2$

Calculation: $0.66 = 6.67 \times 10^{-11}M \times 0.5/(1.57 \times 10^6)^2$

Final answer: $M = 4.9 \times 10^{22}$ kg

MATHEMATICS

Below are two examples of questions assessing primarily memory skills, taken from an elementary school mathematics lesson on data representation. The first is in multiple-choice format, and the second is a short-answer question. In the multiple-choice format, students are asked to circle the correct definition of what a prediction is: (a) a way to collect data, (b) a piece of paper on which people record their response, (c) a type of graph, or (d) before you collect the data, what you think the results will be.

In the short-answer format, students are told: "When you conduct a study, you ask a question, and then you predict what your results will be. What is the next step after predicting your results?" The students are asked to write down their answers.

Table 33 provides another example of an elementary school level assessment of memory skills, this time using figures as the multiple-choice stimuli to choose from. This assessment from a lesson on geometry primarily taps memory skills because unless you remember what the term *perpendicular* means, you cannot answer the question.

Table 33   Elementary School Mathematics Item Primarily Assessing Memory Skills (Geometry)

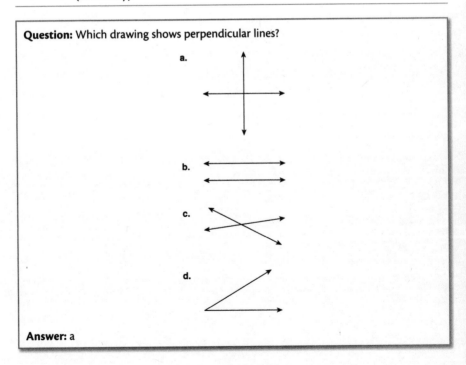

CLOSING ACTIVITY

Now it's your turn! Go back to your lesson overview in Table 28, or think of a particular lesson that you typically teach, and come up with a multiple-choice question to assess students' memory skills. Don't forget to indicate the correct answer!

Question:

_____

_____

_____

a. _____

b. _____

c. _____

d. _____

The correct answer is: _____

14

Assessing and Rating Analytical Skills

As we discussed in Part II, analytical items require students to analyze (e.g., the plot of a story); critique (e.g., the design of a science experiment); evaluate (e.g., whether a certain formula is appropriate for solving a mathematical problem); or compare and contrast (e.g., the attitudes of two characters in a story).

You can write assessment items so that they specifically target a given cognitive skill, such as analytical thinking skills, and then assess students' answers to the extent that they demonstrate the targeted skill in their response. For example, if students are asked to "compare and contrast two systems of government" but provide a very imaginative answer that does not at all address two forms of government, that response would be rated low for analytical thinking. As any experienced teacher knows, however, students' conceptual knowledge displayed in the answer does not always match the form. In other words, some students have good ideas and a great deal of knowledge, but lack spelling, grammar, and punctuation skills.

To get around the problem of letting "form" influence the assessment of thinking skills, we sometimes evaluate students' open-ended responses on two separate dimensions: general accuracy ("form") and ability in the targeted skill (e.g., analytical, creative, or practical), remembering that abilities are fluid rather than fixed. We will show examples of this double rating of both general accuracy and ability/skill in the targeted skill in the illustrations relating to science that follow. It's not always possible or convenient to rate for these two characteristics, however, and sometimes we provide a global rating comprising both accuracy and the extent to which the answer demonstrates analytical, practical, or creative thinking. The language arts and math illustrations come from lessons in which we rated for just a single dimension. We have decided to show examples of the two dimensional ratings in science only for more consistency, but it is possible to evaluate responses in other content areas (language arts, math, social science, second language, art, etc.) on two dimensions as well.

LANGUAGE ARTS

The following is an example of an open-ended question designed to assess analytical skills from a language arts lesson in the literary genre of "wonder tales." Students are given the following task: "You are trying to find out about what hummingbirds eat. You have found two (hypothetical) books: *What to Put in Your Garden Bird Feeders* and *Bird Watching*. Which book do you think is more likely to have the answer to your question? Explain why you think so."

Accurate answers give the title *What to Put in Your Garden Bird Feeders*, but the number of points attributed to the answer will vary on a 0- to 5-point scale, depending on the reasons given and the complexity and level of detail of the answer. In Table 34, we indicate what elements are necessary for an answer to be given—0, 1, 2, 3, 4, or 5 points, respectively—and show sample responses that received these different scores.

Table 34   Rubric for Rating Responses to an Elementary School Language Arts Assessment for Analytical Abilities

Value	Description of Value	Examples of Responses
0	Completely wrong or off-topic.	*Bird Watching* (no reason given); *I think it is a good idea; Dictionary; Bird* (wrong answers with no reasons attempted).
1	Minimal attempt to answer; answer demonstrates little understanding of what the question asks; may merely repeat the question in the answer.	*Bird Watching cause bird watching will tell you all the information* (wrong answer with reason attempted).

Value	Description of Value	Examples of Responses
2	Little evidence of analysis; little or no understanding of how to use the thinking process called for in the question; answer may be vague, formulaic, or appear to have been memorized rather than thought out.	*What to put in Your Garden Bird Feeder because it sounds better* (correct answer with little or no evidence of analysis); *What to Put in your Garden Bird Feeders* (correct answer; no reason given; no analysis).
3	Answer demonstrates some understanding of the thinking process called for in the question but includes an incorrect or partially correct answer or solution; the response may be illogical.	*In Your Garden Bird Feeders because it would tell you what all birds eat* (correct answer, some analysis, logic is not entirely correct because "all birds" are not "garden birds"); *What to Put in Your Garden Bird Feeders because Bird Watching probably tells you about watching birds* (correct answer, some analysis but by "process of elimination" rather than analysis of content of correct book title); (correct answer, illogical reasons).
4	Answer demonstrates basic understanding of the material, uses the appropriate thinking process, and arrives at a satisfactory and logical answer.	*What to put in Your Garden Feeders because what you put in your garden for birds to eat* (answer demonstrates correct analysis although weak in communication); *What to Put... because they are talking about what birds eat.*
5	Answer demonstrates a sophisticated and in-depth understanding of the thinking process called for; the student articulates the thinking involved (e.g., names the process, explains how the problem was solved) and/or goes beyond what the question calls for.	*What to Put in Your Garden Bird Feeders because you could look for a hummingbird and it would tell you what they eat* (answer demonstrates matching of book title and its content as well as an understanding of how to go about finding the information in the book).

SCIENCE

In the science examples here and for those showing how to assess for creative and practical skills, we will illustrate the idea of two-dimensional scoring described above. For greater clarity, we have decided to take all the examples from elementary school science lessons, but this is not to say that you cannot apply two-dimensional scoring in other content areas or at other grade levels. Table 35 describes the general accuracy scale, and Table 36, the specific scale for rating the extent to which the student's response displayed analytical skills. In other words, for each student response to each question, we provide an accuracy rating *and* an analytical rating (or a creative rating or a practical rating, depending on the skill tapped by the question). The rationale is to separate cognitive skill from grammar and spelling. It is possible, for example, for a student to be very creative, or to have good analytical skills, but at the same time to have poor spelling and grammar (due to a lack of schooling, a lack of mastery of the language used in the classroom, a specific learning disability, or some other cause).

Table 36 illustrates how the second rating, the extent to which the student's response demonstrates the targeted cognitive skill (analytical, in this case), is obtained for this same elementary school science lesson.

Table 35 Rubric for Rating Elementary School Students' Responses to Open-Ended Science Questions

Value	Responses
0	Completely wrong and off-topic.
1	Minimal attempt to answer the question; little or no relationship to question asked; "a wild guess."
2	Incorrect answer but related to the question.
3	A partially correct or incomplete answer.
4	Completely correct answer but contains communication errors; answer may be difficult to understand. Content is correct, but information is relayed simply or poorly (i.e., one-word answers or sentence fragments).
5	Clear, complete, and totally accurate answer with no significant communication errors. Answers are elaborate and sophisticated.

Table 36 Rubric for Rating Analytical Skills in Elementary School Students' Responses to a Science Question

Question:
Name one difference between a concave and a convex lens and explain how that characteristic plays out for each type of lens.

Rubric:

Value	Responses
0	Answers completely wrong and off-topic.
1	States only that they are different in shape, spelling, or use OR simply draws the two lenses (e.g., *to show difference in shape*).
2	Gives vague characteristics or does not specify which lens (e.g., *you get a better view with one than the other, one goes in, one goes out; one can help you make a fire, the other can't*).
3	Gives more specific characteristics and specifies whether it is concave or convex (e.g., *a convex lens curves out, a concave lens has a wider beam*).
4	Gives specific physical characteristics of both lenses and specifies which characteristic goes with which lens (e.g., *concave goes in and convex goes out; a convex lens makes light brighter and a concave lens doesn't; you can use a convex lens to make a fire, but not a concave lens; a concave lens is thicker at the edges and thinner in the middle; a convex lens is thinner at the edges and thicker in the middle*).
5	Gives specific uses of both lenses and specifies which use goes with which lens (e.g., *a concave lens makes things smaller when you look through it and a convex lens makes things bigger; a convex lens makes light beams converge and a concave lens makes light beams diverge/diffuse*) OR gives a detailed and labeled drawing of the lenses and light beams.

Analytical skills can also be assessed using the multiple-choice format. Here is an example of a multiple-choice item from a high school science lesson on atoms: Students are asked "Which of the following statements is *not* true?" and are directed to circle the correct answer among the following: (a) electrons are negatively charged, (b) the nucleus is positively charged, (c) the nucleus is composed of neutrons and protons, or (d) a positive charge is always stronger than a negative charge. This is an analytical question rather than a memory question because it requires students to analyze each answer option and relate it to their prior knowledge, as they are unlikely to have memorized a set of facts that are untrue of atoms.

MATHEMATICS

Below is an example of a forced-choice item primarily assessing analytical skills taken from a middle school mathematics lesson on exponents. Students were asked to "Match up the professions below with the kind of measure (expressed with an exponent) you are most likely to use. Draw a line connecting the two."

• a cell biologist	• 10 meters
• an astronomer	• 10^{-7} meters
• a tailor	• 10^2 meters
• a sprinter	• 10^{22} meters

This is primarily an analytical question because students have to evaluate which quantities are most likely to be used by each profession. A cell biologist would not be very helped by 10^{22} meters (also known as light years), but 10^{-7} meters, also known as microns, would be suitable. A sprinter would be interested in quantities around 100 meters (10^2) and a tailor in slightly smaller dimensions.

Table 37 presents an open-ended item tapping into students' analytical skills, accompanied by the corresponding rubric, taken from a high school statistics lesson.

Table 37   Rubric for Rating an Open-Ended Analytical Question From A High School Statistics Lesson

Question:

Compare and contrast the notions of *mean* and *mode*. For a given distribution, are mean and mode always the same thing? Give one common characteristic and one difference between the two.

Rubric:

+ 1 point	If the student answers "no" to the first question.
+ 1 point	If the student gives an example *or* explains why mean and mode are not always the same thing.
+ 1 point	If the student gives one common characteristic (e.g., both measure the central tendency of a distribution).
+ 1 point	If the student gives one difference between the two (e.g., the mean is the average of all values, while the mode is the most frequently found value).
+ 1 point	Bonus for any additional graphs, illustrations, or examples.

CLOSING ACTIVITY

We're once again putting you to the task, but this time we're asking for both one multiple-choice *and* one open-ended assessment question, each targeting analytical thinking skills, in the area you focused on in Table 28 (or another lesson of your choice).

Question 1 [Multiple Choice]:

_____

_____

_____

a. _____

b. _____

c. _____

d. _____

The correct answer is: _____

Question 2 [Open-Ended]:

_____

_____

_____

Describe what key elements you expect in the answer:

_____

_____

_____

_____

Assessing and Rating Creative Skills

Creative items require students to: create (e.g., a comic strip summarizing a story they've read); imagine (e.g., a new ending to a story); invent (e.g., a science experiment); or suppose (e.g., What would happen if everything was twice the size it is now?), as we saw in examples in Part II. When we conduct teacher professional-development workshops, most participants agree that it is a good idea to introduce additional creative activities in the classroom, and at the end of the training session most teachers have come up with their own sample creative activities. Some teachers are concerned about meeting the requirements of the No Child Left Behind Act, but teaching students to think creatively should enhance test scores for students who are creative learners, while helping other students to realize the importance of creative thinking. In general, when it comes to discussing assessment; however, teachers are more reluctant to embrace the value of creative thinking skills. "You can't assess it," "It would be arbitrary, everyone has his or her own definition of creativity," and "Creativity can't be defined," are some of the objections we have encountered. It is possible, though, (a) to develop assessment items that tap primarily into creative skills, and (b) to rate student answers to these questions just as reliably as you rate answers to open-ended analytical or practical questions. In the Appendix to Part I, there are some suggestions for further readings for those of you who are interested in learning more about the theory behind this approach to teaching and assessment. Many of the references also provide examples from past PACE work, demonstrating just how reliably we can assess creative skills in students' work.

Here, we will provide you with plenty of examples to illustrate how you can design a question targeting creative thinking skills and how you can rate students' answers. You will also see examples of forced-choice questions, and we will discuss the particular challenge posed by designing creative multiple-choice questions. (Yes, it is a challenge, but there is a way to do it!)

LANGUAGE ARTS

The following is an example of an open-ended response question in language arts designed to assess creative skills from the elementary school unit, previously mentioned in Chapter 13, called "True Wonders." After having studied the literary genre of wonder tales, students are given the following task in the end-of-unit assessment: "Suppose your teacher assigns a report on a science topic. You have found a great deal of information on your topic. Be imaginative and describe what you can do or make to show what you have learned."

Accurate answers describe products students can make to demonstrate their knowledge of the science topic (e.g., a poster, a report, an article, a children's science book, a news article, or a graphic organizer), or performances (e.g., a presentation, a videotape, panel, or a radio show report). The number of points attributed to the answer will vary, however, on a 0-5 scale, depending on the extent the points are creative, as demonstrated by fluidity and originality of ideas. In Table 38, we indicate what elements are necessary for an answer to be given—0, 1, 2, 3, 4, or 5 points, respectively—and show sample responses that received these different scores.

Table 38   Rubric for Attributing a Score to a Language Arts Creative Assessment Item

Task:

Suppose your teacher assigns a report on a science topic. You have found a great deal of information on your topic. Be imaginative and describe what you can do or make to show what you have learned.

Rubric:

Value	Description of Value	Examples of Responses
0	Completely wrong or off-topic.	*About science; math.*
1	Totally unimaginative answer.	*I went to the internet I printed the thing on my person and I typed my report; look up science on the computer for more information* (no imagination; probably not even an original report).
2	Answer repeats or rephrases information cued by the question; does not respond originally.	*Make a good report; write all of the information; write it in a notepad* (repeats cue; no originality; typical "reports").
3	Answer departs somewhat from the model but is unimaginative and substantially unoriginal.	*Show them a movie* (answer is incomplete; unclear whether the student has produced the movie or has found a movie to show); *do something with the class* (not specific enough to determine originality); *have it on a piece of paper and tell it to someone* (unimaginative).
4	Answer is imaginative and original, although the origin of the new idea may be apparent (from the model).	*I could make a videotape and a book about it; make a puppet show.*
5	Answer significantly departs from cues in the model and is unusual (e.g., one-of-a-kind, infrequently mentioned); an original and unusual answer; answer that is elaborated and extended; completely inventive, imaginative, and innovative.	*Use some wire coiled around a light bulb put the end into a potato to show how it works* (although the communication is weak, student seems to be describing a science project as a product of his/her research).

As you can imagine, it is more difficult to design multiple-choice questions targeting creative skills than it is to design multiple-choice questions targeting memory or analytical abilities. As we mentioned in the introduction to this book, there are no "pure" abilities. An assessment question will necessarily target more than one skill. But, it is possible to design questions so that they *primarily* target one cognitive ability more than others. In order to primarily target creative abilities with a multiple-choice format, we typically construct questions that ask students to imagine that they are in a situation that they have never encountered but that nevertheless is imaginable. For example, questions requiring students to engage in an "imagine that . . ." or "what if . . ." mode of thinking will be considered to tap into more creative skills. The following two questions are examples of forced-choice items that target creative more than analytical or practical thinking skills (with correct answers in italics).

Question A: Suppose that looking for pirate treasure is like eating alphabet soup. How do you look for clues in the soup?

    a. Put a napkin on your lap.

    b. Drink the soup from a cup.

    c. Serve the soup to a friend.

    d. *See if you can spell words with the alphabet letters.*

Question B: In Giant Land everyone is as tall as, or taller, than Abraham Lincoln. Suppose that Lincoln paid a visit to Giant Land. How would Giant Land biographers describe Lincoln's appearance?

    a. Lincoln is a tall, lean person.

    b. *Lincoln is a rather short man.*

    c. When Lincoln took off his stovepipe hat, he still towered over everyone else.

    d. Lincoln towered over the other speakers.

In order to answer these two questions, students have to "think outside the box." They cannot reply on the basis of anything they have studied in class, so they will put their creative thinking skills to use.

SCIENCE

The following example of an open-ended response in science, designed to assess creative skills, is pulled from the same elementary school unit on light we referred to earlier (see Tables 35 and 36). In the end-of-unit assessment, students are given the following task: "Pretend that you have a special friend who happens to be a light beam. Your friend plans to visit you. You want your friend to have a good time, so you design a tour that will enable your friend to experience reflection, refraction, and absorption. Describe three things you would plan for your friend."

The accuracy scale for grading this science assessment was provided in Table 36, under the heading "assessing analytical skills." Table 39 provides the scale to assess the students' answer for creative skill, and we indicate what elements are necessary for an answer to be given—0, 1, 2, 3, 4, or 5 points respectively.

Table 39   Rubric for Rating Creative Ability on an Open-Ended Elementary School Science Creative Assessment Item

Task:

Pretend that you have a special friend who happens to be a light beam. Your friend plans to visit you. You want your friend to have a good time, so you design a tour that will enable your friend to experience reflection, refraction, and absorption. Describe three things you would plan for your friend.

Rubric:

Value	Responses
0	Answers that are completely wrong and off-topic.
1	Things you can do or places you can go with a friend, but that are not related to question (e.g., *go to Arby's, wood cabin, forest without creek*).
2	Items or activities that are appropriate for a friend who is a light beam (e.g., *mirror, glass*).
3	Activities without items (e.g., *reflect, refract, absorb*).
4	Description of activities without mention of the experience OR a list of items with labels of what each item would allow them to experience (e.g., *one room filled with mirrors, another with mirrors and transparent sheets, the last with black fabric; a mirror for reflection, a window for refraction, and a rock for absorption*).
5	Detailed description of activities with explanation of what they would experience.

As noted on page 81 in the section devoted to language arts, it is much more difficult to construct creative multiple-choice items than it is to create open-ended creative questions, or forced-choice questions tapping into memory or analytical skills. But it can be done, and here are a few examples from science lessons (with correct answers in italics).

Question A: Below is a list of metallic objects. If you had a magnet the size of a baseball, circle the metallic objects you would be able to pick up. Circle the answer(s) of your choice.

    a. car

    b. *metal ruler*

    c. refrigerator

    d. *paper clip*

Question B: Imagine you are living at the North Pole. You want your friend to come and visit. He does not know what direction to follow. What instrument would he use to help him find his way?

    a. *compass*

    b. keeper

    c. lodestone

    d. bar magnet

These items primarily target creative thinking because they require students to imagine a novel situation (e.g., having a magnet the size of a baseball, living at the North Pole) in which she or he is unlikely ever to have been.

MATHEMATICS

Let's start with the trickiest part this time, and look at some forced-choice assessment questions targeting primarily creative skills in elementary school students. Again, both items assess creative-thinking skills in that they require students to imagine a potential situation that they never will confront in reality and that they have not previously discussed in class (with correct answers in italics).

Question A: Imagine you found a secret recipe that made you shrink to half your size. What would your arm be closest to in length?

    a. the length of a tree trunk

    b. the length of a paper clip

    c. the length of a giraffe's neck

    d. *the length of a banana*

Question B: Imagine it was bedtime and time started suddenly to go backwards. What things would happen next?

    a. first dinner, then breakfast, then lunch

    b. first breakfast, then lunch, then dinner

    c. *first dinner, then lunch, then breakfast*

    d. first lunch, then breakfast, then dinner

Table 40 provides an example of an open-ended assessment question from a high school lesson on algebra.

Table 40 Open-Ended Assignment for Assessment of Creative Thinking in a High School Mathematics Lesson on Algebra

Background:

By the Renaissance, mathematics had achieved a level of development far beyond the practical problem-solving needs of finance, architecture, or engineering. To arithmetic and geometry, both grounded in association with real quantities, spaces, shapes, and magnitudes, was now added algebra, a branch of mathematics based on purely abstract entities and their properties, relationships, and operations.

    The basic language of algebra is quite simple. Symbols refer to any quantity, set, or type of number, as the operation defines it; parentheses keep the order of operations clear or group certain elements together. A power is identified by a smaller number at its upper right: 5^7 or 3^x or x^y. They are called base and characteristic respectively.

Task:

Algebra has not always been used. Imagine that you were a very gifted mathematician and came up with a new kind of mathematics. What would this new theory be called and what kind of problems would it deal with?

_____

_____

_____

_____

CLOSING ACTIVITY

Your turn! Since multiple-choice questions are often trickier to generate than open-ended questions when it comes to assessing primarily for creative thinking skills, let's start with the easier of the two.

Question 1 [Open-Ended]:

_____

_____

_____

Describe what key elements you expect in the answer:

_____

_____

_____

_____

Question 2 [Multiple Choice]:

_____

_____

_____

a. _____

b. _____

c. _____

d. _____

The correct answer is: _____

This question targets creative thinking skills because it (*complete the sentence*)

_____

_____

_____

16

Assessing and Rating Practical Skills

As we learned in Part II, devoted to teaching activities, tasks associated with practical-thinking skills require students to apply their skills and knowledge to real-world settings. Practical assessment items, for example, require students to apply (e.g., the lesson of a story to a real-life event); use (e.g., a ruler to measure length); or implement what has been learned (e.g., the six big steps in library research: task definition, information seeking strategies, location and access, use of information, synthesis, and evaluation). The creative questions about imaginary countries inhabited by giants, or large numbers being characters in a TV show, which we discussed previously, would not be considered practical!

It is easy to think of performance-based assessments of practical skills, that is, situations in which you ask the student to complete a task or produce something to demonstrate that he or she has acquired the skill you are trying to teach. Here we will give you examples (and the corresponding rubrics) to show how you can develop written assessment items that tap into practical-thinking skills.

LANGUAGE ARTS

In literature classes, we should ask students to relate the material they're reading to their own life. The following is an example of a homework question for high school students reading Harper Lee's (1960) *To Kill a Mockingbird:* "Scout is upset because her teacher tells her not to read anymore. How would you react if your teacher told you not to read? Would it make you happy or would it upset you? Explain why."

Another example of a practical activity (taken from a different lesson) is one in which students have to figure out how to find an answer to the problem: "Your cousin has just been assigned a report on inventions. She thinks that her first step should be to look up *invention* in the encyclopedia. What advice would you give her about what she should do first?"

Accurate answers indicate that students are able to recognize that they need to narrow down the topic as the first step (e.g., a particular invention, or the top twenty inventions of the century, etc). The number of points attributed to the answer will vary, however, on a 0–5 scale, depending on the sophistication of the answer. In Table 41, we indicate what elements are necessary for an answer to be given—0, 1, 2, 3, 4, or 5 points respectively—and show sample responses that received these different scores.

Table 41   Rubric for a Language Arts Assessment Primarily Addressing Practical Skills

Task:

Your cousin has just been assigned a report on inventions. She thinks she should start by looking up *invention* in the encyclopedia. What advice would you give her about what she should do first?"

Value	Rubric	Examples of Responses
0	Completely wrong or off-topic.	*Envelops.*
1	Minimal or no attempt to solve the problem; no attempt to relate the problem to a real-life situation; minimal relation to the question.	*Read the encyclopedia; look in the encyclopedia; the same as she said; a book; she start it; read invention* (no attempt to solve the problem; repeats information in the question).
2	Attempt to solve the problem but the solution is not very practical and may be inappropriate; does not take the context into account; ignores relevant information in the problem.	*Look under the letter I read it write it on a typewriter then you are done* (ignores relevant information, i.e., the cousin probably knows how to use an encyclopedia; her question was about where to start); *look in the index* (not a helpful answer, e.g., in which book?); *look in an atlas* (inappropriate solution).

(Continued)

(Continued)

Value	Rubric	Examples of Responses
3	Answer demonstrates some understanding of the problem; answer offers an inefficient or incomplete solution; uses only information in the question and does not draw upon tacit knowledge or previous experience or answers from general knowledge without applying it to the situation described in the question; answer may be vague and lacking specific details.	*Go on your computer and find a book on inventions; get a book on inventions; go to the card catalog and look up people; check out a book on inventions* (suggests strategies to learn about inventions or do library research, but impractical because the student has not narrowed a broad topic).
4	Answer demonstrates basic understanding of the problem situation and how to go about its solution; answer makes a connection to personal or real-life experiences.	*Think of an invention to do* (an accurate answer but not necessarily helpful to someone having difficulty getting started).
5	Answer demonstrates thorough understanding of the problem and connects the new material to personally relevant real-life experiences for the practical application of knowledge; answer makes use of information particular to the situation; highly contextualized; answer demonstrates a keen awareness of human nature and the common good; answer may go beyond self-interest.	*Pick an invention you're interested in* (practical advice, relating to researcher's interests); *tell her about how somebody invented something* (a helpful suggestion, gives an example; may possibly be "advice" student him/herself was given by a teacher to help spark interest in a topic—an example of a student learning "practical" intelligence tacitly).

Questions A and B illustrate multiple-choice items primarily assessing practical thinking skills.

Question A: If you wanted to assuage your younger brother's fear of ghosts, you should (This question follows a lesson in which students have learned that the meaning of the word "assuage" is to calm, to reduce, or to mollify.)

   a. take him to a horror movie
   b. *calmly explain that ghosts don't exist*
   c. dress up as a ghost and scare him
   d. talk to your parents about it

Question B: If you wanted to experience living conditions close to those of many Transcendentalist writers, you should (This question follows a lesson in which students have discussed the Transcendentalist movement in U.S. literature.)

   a. move to a skyscraper in New York
   b. *move to the countryside*
   c. move to the suburbs
   d. move to a hotel

SCIENCE

The following example of an open-ended response designed to assess practical skills in science is also pulled from the unit on light. In the end-of-unit assessment, students are given the following task: "List two practical uses for mirrors besides looking at yourself in them."

In Table 42, we indicate what elements are necessary for an answer to be graded—0, 1, 2, 3, 4, or 5 points, respectively.

Question A is another example from the science unit on light, using multiple-choice format to assess practical skills. It is practical in that it requires students to think of a situation that they might already have faced—or are likely to face—in their own lives.

Table 42 Rubric for a Middle School Science Assessment Primarily Addressing Practical Skills

Task:
List two practical uses for mirrors besides looking at your own reflection.

Rubric:

Value	Responses
0	Answers that are completely wrong and off-topic.
1	Help you look good, holding it and reflecting it (doesn't specify "it"), make light, reflecting and absorbing, looking at your hair/suit.
2	Funhouse mirror, for decoration, putting makeup on, shaving.
3	Reflect light, find secret messages and codes, see things behind you.
4	Look at the back of your head, kaleidoscope, make a room look bigger.
5	Look behind yourself when you're in a car, spying and looking at other people, reflect light to make fires or signals, periscope, telescope, camera.

Question A: You plan to have a slumber party and want the least amount of light necessary to read a spooky story. What light source would you use? Circle one.

    a. sunlight

    b. *large flashlight*

    c. overhead lights (the ones you switch on with a light switch)

    d. a lamp with a bright light bulb

Question B is taken from a different lesson, this one for high school students and focusing on atoms, requiring students to make the lesson more concrete by relating it to their everyday experience. It is not a multiple-choice item, but rather, a short-answer item with limited answer options. Question C, on the other hand, is a straightforward multiple-choice item.

Question B: Find something in your everyday life that illustrates the relation between atoms and matter:

Atoms are to matter what _____ are to _____.

Question C: If you put a silver spoon into boiling water and hold on to it, you will

- a. feel cold
- b. not feel anything
- c. feel slightly warm
- d. *burn yourself*

MATHEMATICS

Table 43 provides an example of a student assignment that primarily requires practical skills. In assessing student responses, the teacher will take into account (1) the extent to which students have truly selected a phenomenon from their daily life, and (2) the extent to which students use proper mathematical notations.

Table 43 Open-Ended Assignment Primarily Tapping Into Students' Practical Skills (from a high school mathematics lesson on properties of exponents)

Task:

Think of something you do every day, and have been doing every day for most of your life. It can be any trivial action, like brushing your teeth, smiling to greet your friends, or listening to CDs.

Calculate how many times a day you perform this action, then estimate how many times you do it in a month, then in a year, and finally how many times you are likely to have done it in your life.

Express these results using the scientific notations you have learned in this section.

The action I am thinking of:

Calculations and scientific notation:

Questions A and B give some sample multiple-choice items assessing primarily practical thinking skills, in that they describe situations that students may have faced, or could very well face in the future, in their own lives.

Question A: In order to decide in which supermarket to buy your food, you should buy the same products in different stores and then look at:

a. the average bill, considering all shops together
b. *the total bill, considering each shop individually*
c. the range of bills
d. the median bill, considering all shops

Question B: Your family is moving and you need some boxes in which to pack your things. One of the most important things you want to pack is your computer monitor. In which shaped box would it be best to pack your computer monitor?

a. *a cube*
b. a cone
c. a pyramid
d. a sphere

CLOSING ACTIVITY

By now, you probably know what to expect when you see the words "Closing Activity"; that's right; it's time for you to apply what you've learned!

Question 1 [Multiple Choice]:

_____

_____

_____

a. _____

b. _____

c. _____

d. _____

The correct answer is: _____

This question targets practical thinking skills because it (*complete the sentence*)

_____

_____

_____

Question 2 [Open-Ended]:

_____

_____

_____

Describe what key elements you expect in the answer:

_____

_____

_____

_____

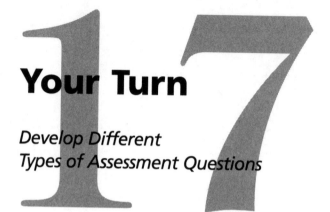

Your Turn

*Develop Different
Types of Assessment Questions*

n this part of the book we have tried to show you (1) how important it
is to match teaching and assessment, and (2) how you can assess
students' skills and knowledge through a range of thinking skills (memory, analytical, creative, and practical). We have also given you an opportunity to develop some questions of your own, addressing these different
thinking skills. Some of you may have had the added benefit of working
with a colleague to brainstorm questions and balance ideas around why
a given question is more likely to assess memory, analytical, creative, or
practical thinking skills. In concluding Part III, we would like you to move
up to the next step and actually try out these techniques in your classroom. Generate an open-ended question (or take one you've developed
throughout the closing activities to each chapter), give it to your students,
and collect their answers. As you initially developed these questions, we
asked you to think of the important elements you would want to see in
student responses. Now we invite you to develop more detailed rubrics,
both for general accuracy and for the specific thinking skill that you are
assessing. Table 44 will guide you through this activity, and you will see
that it is similar in format to those we have used as illustrations; so do not
hesitate to go back and review those again. Have fun!

Table 44   Develop Your Own Rubric With Sample Student Responses

Write your question here: _____

_____

_____

This question primarily assesses Memory/Analytical/Creative/Practical thinking skills (*circle one*)

Accuracy Scale

Value	Description of Value	Sample Responses
0	Completely wrong or off-topic.	
1	Minimal attempt to answer the question; little or no relationship to question asked; "a wild guess."	
2	Incorrect answer but related to the question.	
3	A partially correct or incomplete answer.	
4	Completely correct answer but contains communication errors; answer may be difficult to understand.	
5	Clear, complete, and totally accurate answer with no significant communication errors; answers are elaborated and sophisticated.	

(Continued)

Table 44 (Continued)

Proficiency scale in the following thinking skill: _____
(Make sure it matches the thinking skill you circled above.)

Value	Description of Value	Sample Responses
0		
1		
2		
3		
4		
5		

NOTE

1. Advanced Placement (A.P.) courses are offered to advanced high school students in certain schools and sanctioned by an exam that is common to all A.P. students of that subject matter, contrary to most other assessments in U.S. schools which are specific to the school, the district, or the state, rather than national in scope.

PART IV

Why and How to Teach for Wisdom

Introduction to Teaching for Wisdom

So far, we have talked about the importance of broadening your teaching and assessment repertoire to reach a range of learners and to help all the students in your classroom succeed by capitalizing on their strengths and compensating for their weaknesses. It's important that all students be given the opportunity to learn, to grow intellectually, to pursue an education, or to be able to find the job of their dreams. To become fully successful members of the human community, however, our students also need to develop wisdom-based thinking skills. In life, we all face difficult everyday problems, and to be successful in life means to be able to solve these difficult and uncertain everyday life problems, in which we have to rely on wisdom to make the right decision. In Part IV, we will describe how we define wisdom and wisdom-based thinking, but let's first review situations when wisdom-related thinking is needed.

For example, as children, we can be exposed to seeing other children picking on someone, and we need to decide how to deal with that. How do you best react—both to protect yourself and to make sure the child being picked on is not worse off because of your intervention? As young adults, we are confronted with all the difficult problems of intimate relationships. How do you act when the partner you have fallen for is not accepted by your family? Which do you choose when your education or career threatens your romantic relationship? As older adults, most of us have to worry about caring for both our children and our parents. As your parents become less able to take care of themselves, how do you best care for them?

We could cite an endless list of difficult everyday choices that one is exposed to during the course of a lifetime, and you can probably think of quite a few as well. If one of the roles of schooling is to give students the knowledge and cognitive tools that they will need to succeed in life, then we believe that school *should* help enhance wisdom-based thinking skills in students. As educators, we have a responsibility to see to it that our students put their intelligence, knowledge, and skills to good use—toward bettering the lives of all rather than just advancing their own personal agendas. We believe that teachers can help their students in positive development by modeling wise behavior and teaching wisdom-based thinking skills. Part IV will first describe three types of wisdom-based thinking skills, and then we will review six general principles for teaching and modeling wisdom in the classroom in different content areas. We will show detailed examples from a social science curriculum we developed into which we infused these wisdom-based thinking skills.

Table 45 summarizes why we believe it is important to teach our students wisdom-based thinking skills. At the end of the chapter, you'll have a chance to reflect on these general guidelines and to think of how they might apply in your own classroom.

Table 45 Four Reasons Why Schools Should Include Instruction in Wisdom-Based Thinking Skills in Their Curriculum

1. First, knowledge is insufficient for wisdom and certainly does not guarantee satisfaction or happiness. Wisdom seems a better vehicle to the attainment of these goals.

2. Second, wisdom provides a mindful and considered way to enter thoughtful and deliberative values into important judgments. One cannot be wise and at the same time be impulsive or mindless in one's judgments.

3. Third, wisdom represents an avenue to creating a better, more harmonious world. Dictators such as Adolph Hitler and Joseph Stalin may have been knowledgeable and may even have been good critical thinkers, at least with regard to the maintenance of their own power. Given the definition of wisdom, however, it would be hard to argue they were wise.

4. Fourth and finally, students—who later may become parents and leaders—are always part of a greater community and hence will benefit from learning to judge rightly, soundly, or justly on behalf of their community.

Three Wisdom-Based Thinking Skills

In Part I of this book, we described the balance theory of wisdom, and gave our definition of wisdom. To refresh your memory, the balance theory of wisdom posits that wise thinking involves the ability to use one's knowledge, intelligence, and creativity in the service of a common good by balancing one's own interests with those of other people and of a broader community, through the infusion of positive ethical values, over both the short and the long terms. How can this theoretical model be translated into guidelines for the classroom? We need to provide students with educational contexts in which they can formulate their own understanding of what constitutes wise thinking. In other words, teaching for wisdom is not accomplished by telling students *about wisdom*, but rather, by letting students actively experience wise decision making. Toward this end, teachers can provide scaffolding for the development of wisdom and case studies to help students develop wisdom, but a teacher cannot teach particular courses of actions or give students a list of dos and don'ts.

What we can do, however, is to encourage students to develop three wisdom-based thinking skills: (1) thinking reflectively, (2) thinking dialogically, and (3) thinking dialectically. Let's describe each one of these thinking skills and give some classroom examples.

When students engage in *reflective thinking*, they reflect on their own functioning to increase their metacognition, that is, their awareness of their own thoughts and beliefs. Reflective thinking can enhance wise thinking because, in order to make a wise decision, one needs to come up with a strategy, monitor how successful the chosen strategy is, and modify it if it is not successful, finding strategies that better fit the situational demands. This monitoring requires reflective thinking. Teachers can help students to practice reflective thinking by designing instructional activities that allow students to explore and shape their own values. Also, students can be explicitly instructed in useful metacognitive strategies, such as self-questioning or the use of self-monitoring checklists. Table 46 provides one such checklist for students as an example, but there are many others available in printed or online resource libraries. You can encourage your students to be more self-reflective in any content area, and the sample checklist can be equally well used in a mathematics, social science, foreign language, or language arts classroom.

Table 46 Reflective Thinking: Self-Monitoring Checklist for Students

1. What is the problem or task at hand?

2. What resources do I need to allocate to solve the problem?
   o Time?
   o Material resources (books, pens, rulers, calculator, maps)?
   o Collaborative resources (guidance from a teacher, from a peer)?
   o Informational resources (library, Internet)?

3. How can I mentally represent the problem so that it makes sense?

4. What is the best strategy for solving the problem or completing the task?

5. (Once problem solving starts) Is my problem solving making sense? Am I on the right track? (Once problem solving is completed) Did I solve the problem? Did I solve it correctly? If not, what did I do wrong and how could I do it differently next time?

When students engage in *dialogical thinking*, they take into account different frames of reference and various perspectives to find the best possible solution for all parties involved in the issue. What may at first appear as the right answer may turn out to be the wrong choice when the long term is considered, or when the interest of the community as a whole rather than that of just one individual is taken into account. In the classroom, you can offer activities that encourage *dialogical thinking*, that is, activities in which students have to consider multiple points of view and various perspectives on the issue at hand. You can show your students how optimal solutions come from careful weighing of alternatives, rather than from following one single predetermined or prescribed course of action.

For example, literature is often taught in terms of the standards and context of today, and students judge characters in books and plays by our contemporary standards rather than by the standards of the time and place in which the characters lived and the events surrounding them occurred. A different approach, involving dialogical thinking, would be to encourage students to approach the study of literary works in the context of the time in which they were written. For example, when women are referred to as delicate and feeble creatures in nineteenth century novels, this reference reflects the then societal perception of women being less capable than men. One point of view is to say that we should not read books that are gender biased, but another is to acknowledge the perception of gender changes over time.

The foreign language classroom is another landscape for enhancing students' wisdom-based thinking skills. Foreign languages should be taught in the cultural context in which they are embedded, requiring students to engage in reflective and dialogical thinking truly to grasp the foreign culture and to position themselves and their experiences in relation to this culture. We would do our students a service by teaching them to understand other cultures, rather than just to expect people from other cultures to understand us. Different cultures have different value systems, and you cannot understand culture X if you try to read it through the lens of culture Y. Learning the language of a culture is a key to understanding that culture, and the two should not be taught separately. Nor should culture be viewed as an appendix to language rather than as the context in which language is deeply rooted. Esperanto, a language that was once proposed as a means of promoting communication across cultures, failed. Its failure was largely a result of its being embedded in no culture at all.

In some cases, a given language is shared by very different cultures, making the task more complex (though not impossible!) for the teacher. Spanish, for example, is spoken in cultures as varied as Spain (Europe), Mexico (North America), and Equatorial Guinea (Africa), whereas Japanese is mostly spoken in Japan.

In our history curriculum, one example of an activity that fosters the development of dialogical thinking comes from the historical topic of British colonial polices in the late-eighteenth century. In this activity, students read multiple accounts (primary historical sources) of events during the Boston Massacre. The reports include an excerpt from a colonial newspaper, an account by a British captain, and an interview with a

Boston shoemaker. Students discuss the origins of the differences among the accounts and evaluate the relative credibility of the sources. They are also invited to write their own account of the events of the Boston Massacre and to consider how their own frames of reference affect their descriptions. From this activity, students learn to appreciate the importance of multiple standpoints, the constructed nature of knowledge, and the powerful influences of one's perspective on one's view of the world. Wisdom requires one to see things not only from the standpoint of one's own interests, but also from the standpoint of the interests of others.

When students engage in *dialectical thinking*, they strive to integrate different points of view. Whereas dialogical thinking involves the consideration of multiple points of view, *dialectical thinking* emphasizes the consideration and *integration* of two opposing perspectives. In a way, when you engage in dialectical thinking you become your own "devil's advocate": First, you take one position, and then its opposite. For example, let's say you're an absolute pacifist opposed to any military intervention, whatever the circumstances. Now consider a second perspective, which goes against your first: one can argue that a nation can live freely and in peace only if its borders are protected by armed forces. Now, how can you come up with a *synthesis*, a reconciliation of the two seemingly opposing statements? You can, for example, decide that borders under dispute should be protected by a third party (e.g., an international army), rather than having the opposing countries measure their military strength against each other.

Another example is that one can be firmly opposed to animal cruelty (thesis), while others argue for the necessary use of animals in research (antithesis). A synthesis can be found by agreeing that no animals be used for cosmetic research, but that the limited use of animals is allowed when the research is likely to lead to a cure for a deadly disease (in animals or humans).

The process does not stop, however, when the two opposing views are reconciled; on the contrary, each synthesis becomes a new thesis, which can then be integrated into a new round of dialectical thinking. In the classroom, dialectical thinking can be encouraged through opportunities to study different sources, enabling students to build their own knowledge, or through writing assignments that explicitly call for a thesis, antithesis, and synthesis.

Let's look at an example. In science teaching, dialectical thinking can be applied to illustrate to students the notion that scientific facts are not "true and forever true," but rather, reflect our knowledge at a given moment in time. Many students think of science as the final outcome of a process of exploration and thought, but it is really a dynamic process, and many of the theories and interpretations that we teach in classrooms today will eventually be superseded. The earth was believed for a long time to be flat before it became accepted that it is roughly spherical.

Another example of an activity in which students get to practice their dialectical thinking can be found in our history curriculum on the colonial independence movement in America. Students first study the writings of Thomas Paine and Charles Inglis, who express two opposing views on the question of whether America should break away from England (with Paine, pro, and Inglis, con). Then they consider a compromise solution proposed by Joseph Galloway, who attempted to reconcile the two conflicting positions by suggesting that the union of colonies be governed by a president appointed by the Crown. Students then discuss the notion of compromise and propose their own resolutions to the British-American conflict. Through this activity, students practice synthesizing an opposing perspective, and learn to recognize that the same questions can be answered differently at different points in time.

Six General Guidelines for Teaching Wisdom

In Table 47, we have summarized six general guidelines for modeling and teaching wisdom in the classroom. It is likely that you follow some of these guidelines already. What we strive for in our curriculum is not so much to revolutionize teaching and make instructors rotate their educational practices 180 degrees, but rather, to help teachers systematically and frequently implement sound teaching procedures that foster wise thinking.

We will review each one of these guidelines in more detail below and provide some detailed examples of how they can be applied in the classroom. The detailed examples are all excerpts from two units we developed for use in middle school U.S. history classrooms. The curriculum materials cover the period in American history from colonial times to the creation of the Constitution, emphasizing the diversity of the American experience. This is not to say that wisdom is limited to history—wisdom-based thinking skills can be infused in most subject areas and at most grade levels. Although it may be difficult to engage very young children in dialogical thinking, most of these guidelines can be adapted from the end of elementary school, upward.

Table 47 Six General Guidelines for Teaching Wisdom

1.	Encourage students to read classic works of literature and philosophy to learn and reflect on the wisdom of the sages.
2.	Engage students in class discussions, projects, and essays that encourage them to discuss the lessons they have learned from these works and how they can be applied to their own lives and the lives of others. Particular emphasis should be placed on dialogical and dialectical thinking.
3.	Encourage students to study not only "truth," but values, as developed during their reflective thinking.
4.	Place an increased emphasis on critical, creative, and practical thinking in the service of the common good.
5.	Encourage students to think about how almost *any* topic they study might be used for better or for worse ends and about how important that final end is.
6.	Remember that you, as a teacher, are a role model! To role model wisdom, adopt a Socratic approach to teaching and invite your students to play a more active role in constructing learning—from their own point of view and from that of others.

GUIDELINE #1

Encourage students to read classic works of literature and philosophy to learn and reflect on the wisdom of the sages.

Generally speaking, it's a good idea to encourage students to read classic works of literature and philosophy from different cultures to learn and reflect on the wisdom of the sages. You can encourage students in this way no matter what your content area is. A math teacher *is* allowed to recommend books other than math textbooks! A physical education teacher or coach *can* encourage students to develop a healthy mind in a healthy body by suggesting readings.

Let's look at an example from the history curriculum we developed, in which students study the ideas of the intellectual movement of the

Enlightenment and the character of Benjamin Franklin. In one lesson, students first read Franklin's maxims, such as "Whatever is begun in anger ends in shame," "Be slow in choosing a friend, slower in changing," "Well done is better than well said," and so on (Franklin, 1988 version). Next, students worked in pairs to describe to their partners their own past experiences where one of Franklin's maxims could apply. Students were then invited to think of a maxim that they had learned from their own past and to continue writing their maxims in a notebook or a journal throughout the school year. How did this lesson enhance wisdom-based thinking skills? It did so primarily by engaging students in reflective thinking, and showing them the benefits of reflecting on one's life experiences and thinking about a general rule or maxim they can apply to new situations. Wisdom involves an ability to learn from the past, whether our own or that of other people. By asking students to continue to generate their own maxims throughout the year, we encourage them to turn reflective thinking into a habit of mind.

GUIDELINE #2

Engage students in class discussions, projects, and essays that encourage them to draw lessons from what they learn and apply these lessons to their own lives and the lives of others. Promote dialogical and dialectical thinking.

Engage students in class discussions or projects that encourage them to discuss the lessons they've learned from literary and philosophical works they have read, or from the press and other media, and show them how these lessons can be applied to their own lives. In almost any subject area, we can point out relationships between lessons learned in the classroom and how they apply to the students' (and our own) lives. For example, in history, you can tie historical lessons to personally relevant everyday experiences, as we did in a lesson in which students examined Benjamin Franklin's accomplishments to improving his community (e.g., such as the establishment of a post office and a library), and then considered the needs of our own classroom community and devised a plan to address these needs. As another example, in science class, you can discuss the ancient belief that the Earth is the center of the universe, with the sun and moon circling around it, to stress the importance of the scientific method in providing proof and evidence in support of a given theory or hypothesis. Or you could discuss Galileo's trial and encourage students to think about what they would do if their research led them to conclusions that contradicted the established way of thinking in their community.

GUIDELINE #3

Encourage students to study not only facts, but positive ethical values, as developed during their reflective thinking.

Encourage students to study not only "truth," but positive ethical values, as developed during their reflective thinking. In our history curriculum on the American independence movement, as previously mentioned, students were presented with Benjamin Franklin's maxims and encouraged to engage in reflective thinking. In the homework related to that classroom activity, students were asked to study an excerpt from Franklin's autobiography in which Franklin describes his plan to achieve moral perfection. Having read Franklin's plan, students chose three values that they consider important and then developed their own plan to improve their characters. They were encouraged to monitor their behavior for a week by keeping a journal to record their successes and failures at practicing the chosen values. This activity allows students to explore, form, and apply their own values. Also, students are given an opportunity to monitor events in their daily lives and to recognize the connections between values and actions. Table 48 presents the teaching materials (teacher instruction, classroom transparencies, student worksheets) pertaining to this lesson.

Table 48 Activity From Lesson on Values

<table>
<tr><td colspan="2" align="center">*What Do You Value?*</td></tr>
<tr><td>**Estimated Time**</td><td>20 minutes</td></tr>
<tr><td>**Grouping**</td><td>None</td></tr>
<tr><td>**Presentation Materials**</td><td>Transparency</td></tr>
<tr><td>**Student Materials**</td><td>Worksheet</td></tr>
<tr><td>**Objectives**</td><td>Students will examine the concept of values, an important component of wise thinking.

Students will recognize the connection between actions and values.</td></tr>
</table>

Teacher Instructions:

a. Tell students that they will now work on developing their wise thinking. Write the word "value" on the board. Have students work in pairs and write their own definitions of the word "value" and an example of a value. Have students bring their definitions and examples to the board and post them.

b. Read some of the students' definitions and examples. Then, have students consider the definition and examples that you provide them with. Communicate to students that values are the standards and beliefs that people personally consider worthwhile and desirable. For example, Benjamin Franklin had a value of being a hard worker and he tried to live his life according to this value.

c. The important thing to realize about values is that people have a variety of values, and that different people have different values. Values have a direct effect on people's behaviors. By examining people's values we can better understand their actions and decisions. For example, Benjamin Franklin's praise of hard work is reflected in his many accomplishments. He was a prolific writer, an industrious inventor and scientist, an influential statesman, and a successful businessman who retired from business as a millionaire.

d. Have students examine paintings of a young and an older Benjamin Franklin (you can find pictures on the Internet). Ask students what values appear to characterize Franklin's behaviors as reflected in these paintings. Some possible answers include valuing education, reading, and hard work. These values stayed with him throughout his life.

(Continued)

(Continued)

Transparency

Defining Values

A **value** is a principle, standard, or quality considered worthwhile or desirable. Values are related to our sense of what is right and wrong.

   Examples of values include such qualities as honesty, diligence, compassion, loyalty, respect, responsibility, courage, and generosity.

- Which of Benjamin Franklin's values are being reflected in both of the paintings?
- What details in the pictures helped you to determine your answer?
- Do these paintings confirm or question what you already know about Franklin?

Worksheet

Defining Values

Activities

- How do you understand the word "value"? Write down your definition in the space below. Give an example of a value.

A value is:

_____

_____

_____

An example of a value is:

_____

_____

_____

At first glance it may seem easier to think of examples of how to encourage students to consider ethical values in the philosophy, history, or social sciences classroom, but this guideline can also be applied in language arts, second language, or while discussing the sciences and their use and possible misuse in society. For example, in the biology classroom, there is plenty of opportunity to discuss ethical values in relation to medical research, such as in the debate currently surrounding research using human stem cells. For some people, the value of human life, at its earliest stages, is such that stem cells should never be used, whereas for others, the possible benefits if stem cells could be used to cure severe diseases outweigh the value of protecting an embryo.

GUIDELINE #4

Place an increased emphasis on critical, creative, and practical thinking in the service of the common good.

In previous parts of this book, we have discussed the importance of engaging students in activities that lead them to go beyond the content they have studied (thereby demonstrating creative thinking) and to apply this knowledge to their environment (thereby showing proof of practical thinking), in addition to developing students' memory and analytical thinking skills. To enhance wise thinking, however, students should also be encouraged to consider the outcome of their thinking and actions and to keep in mind that the best solution is not the one that benefits only the individual doing the thinking, but rather, the one that helps others as well. Students should also be encouraged to weigh short-term gain versus longer-term consequences. The guiding principle in choosing between different possible solutions should always be that of the common good.

One example of how we applied this fourth guideline in our history curriculum is that, when studying a unit called "How Slavery Arrived in the New World," students were encouraged to consider the various reasons underlying the choice of importing slaves to work on the sugarcane plantations. Through readings and classroom discussions, students learned about the different reasons behind the Europeans' choice to import free labor from Africa and were asked to debate the analytical reasons for this choice, and to show the limitations of choices made purely on the basis of self-interest: importing free labor may have furthered the goal of increased power and financial wealth for the European settlers, but was it the best solution for the need for more plantation workers? Table 49 contains materials (teacher instructions, classroom transparencies, and student worksheets) from another history lesson, entitled "European Attitudes Toward Locals."

Table 49 Activity From the Unit "How Slavery Arrived in the New World"

European Attitudes Toward Locals	
Estimated Time	20 minutes
Grouping	Small groups (4–6 participants)
Presentation Materials	Transparency
Student Materials	Reading Sheet, Worksheet
Content Objectives	Students will analyze the writing of Christopher Columbus, which depicts his attitudes toward the local population.
Critical Thinking Objectives	Students will identify unstated assumptions. Students will formulate appropriate questions. Students will evaluate the credibility of historical evidence.

Teacher Instructions:

a. Explain to students that many European explorers obviously believed it was their right to take over other people's lands, change their lives, and, if needed, conquer and force them into labor.

b. Divide students into small groups and give them the reading sheet. Have students read the excerpts from Columbus's letter to King Ferdinand and Queen Isabella of Spain, which he sent back to Europe upon his arrival in the new lands in the Caribbean.

c. Have students complete the activities on the worksheet. Students should understand that Columbus assumes that European ways of living, including work, dress, and customs, are superior to those of the natives. He further assumes that it is appropriate to force the native populations to adopt European ways. Students can challenge Columbus's assumptions by reflecting on (1) what makes one way of living better than another, (2) whether it is ever appropriate to change the ways other people live, (3) whether assuming that one's way is better leads to understanding and peaceful relationships among people, and (4) whether there are dangers in not assessing a situation from several perspectives (i.e., not only the European perspective, but also the view of the locals).

d. Have groups report their answers to the class.

e. Evaluate the credibility of the information presented by Columbus in his writings. Use the transparency to present questions to the class: Is it a primary or a secondary source? How large is the lapse of time between the described events and the reporting? Does Columbus ever reflect the point of view of the locals? Was the accuracy of Columbus's account affected by the fact that he did not try to reflect the perspectives of the locals in his descriptions? Did he write his description using a systematic, deliberate process? Did Columbus have motivation (i.e., his religious or political beliefs) to distort the information?

Transparency

Questioning the Credibility of Columbus's Accounts

- Is it a primary or a secondary source?
- How large is the lapse of time between the described events and the reporting?
- Does Columbus ever reflect the point of view of the locals?
- Was the accuracy of Columbus's account affected by the fact that he did not try to reflect the perspectives of the locals?
- Did he write his description using a systematic, deliberate process?
- Did Columbus have motivation (i.e., his religious or political beliefs) to distort the information?

Reading Sheet

European Attitudes Toward Locals

From Christopher Columbus's letter to King Ferdinand and Queen Isabella of Spain.

"Let your majesties be informed that Hispaniola is as much their possession as Castile; they need do nothing more than to have a settlement built here.... These people are most tractable, and easily led; they could be made to sow crops and build cities, and be taught to wear clothes and adopt our customs...

[These people are] "extraordinarily timid.... But once their fear has left them, they give proof of an innocence and a generosity that can scarcely be believed. No matter what is asked of them, they never refuse it, and show themselves contented with any gift offered them.... They are people of noble bearing....

"These people are very unskilled in arms... with fifty men they could all be subjected and made to do all that I wished."

(Continued)

(Continued)

<table>
<tr><td align="center">**Worksheet**</td></tr>
</table>

European Attitudes Toward Locals

Questions

1. In the space below, use your own words to describe the way Columbus viewed the local inhabitants.

   _____

   _____

   _____

2. According to Columbus, what kind of relationship should the Europeans have with the locals?

   _____

   _____

   _____

3. What does Columbus take for granted when he says that the locals "could be made to sow crops and build cities, and be taught to wear clothes and adopt our customs"? List the unstated assumptions that are evident from the above excerpt. Do you agree with Columbus's assumptions?

4. If you could interview Columbus today, what questions would you ask him to challenge his opinions about the native populations and their treatment by Europeans?

   _____

   _____

   _____

Another example of an activity in our history curriculum where students were encouraged to consider the good outcome of their thinking and actions was one centered on the use of different strategies (rational argumentation versus emotional reasoning) to convince others. This activity was a follow-up to a history lesson in which students studied George Whitefield, a very popular Methodist minister from England, who, in the fall of 1739, conducted a series of very dramatic revivals throughout the colonies, involving appealing to participants' emotions. Students were encouraged to draw lessons from this event by relating it to the contemporary world that they live in and the use of arguments and emotions in advertisements. Table 50 provides all the instructional materials (teacher instructions, classroom transparencies, and student worksheets) for this lesson.

Table 50   Activity on the Use of Arguments Versus Emotions in Convincing Others

A Good Kind of Argument	
Estimated Time	20 minutes
Grouping	None
Presentation Materials	Transparencies (2)
Student Materials	None
Objectives	Students will discuss the risks of relying on emotions when making important decisions.
	Students will examine the structure of a rational argument.

Teacher Instructions:

a. Ask students to think of the examples of people using appeals to emotions in modern times. Examples may include political speeches or advertising.

b. Use the first transparency to show some of the slogans used by popular brand names when advertising their products. Ask students what kinds of emotions are being targeted by these slogans. Examples may include: feeling special, belonging to a group, promises of pleasure or happiness.

c. Discuss with students the danger of acting solely upon emotions when making a decision. Students should understand that commercials are aimed at evoking emotions that will make people buy certain products. They often offer no evidence that their claims are, in fact, true. Thus, people may make the decision to buy a product based on *how they feel*, rather than on accurate information.

d. Ask students why emotional or impulsive decision making can be harmful. Explain to students that relying on emotions can lead people to make decisions that are not good for them. Blinded by emotions, people can overlook important information. For example, a commercial might show a beautiful woman happily smoking a cigarette. Inspired by this commercial, a person might buy cigarettes and start smoking. However, medical studies have shown that, instead of leading to happiness, smoking increases the risks of cancer and other diseases. This is why it is important to distinguish between claims that are supported by appeals to emotions and those that are supported by good reasons and evidence. That is, it is important to learn what a *rational argument* is.

(Continued)

(Continued)

e. Tell students that the word *argument* does not necessarily mean a fight or a conflict. People engage in arguments when they want to draw conclusions based on reasons and evidence. Good friends can have arguments when they discuss important questions. They can help each other to think rationally.

f. Use the second transparency to explain the structure of a *rational argument*. Rational arguments are based on reasons and evidence, not on emotions. People should use rational arguments for making decisions. In a rational argument, a claim that something is true is supported by valid reasons. Reasons in rational arguments are further supported with reliable evidence. In a good rational argument, people will also raise objections and will respond to these objections. In the following activity students will examine each part of the argument in greater detail.

Transparency 1

Appeal to Emotions: Modern Advertisement

Brand and Product	Advertising Slogan	Emotion Inspired
Revlon Lipstick	Be unforgettable!	
Mitsubishi Cars	Are you in?	
Skechers' Shoes	Pure Fun!	
Virginia Slims' Cigarettes	It's a woman thing!	
Pepsi Drink	For those who think young!	
L'Oreal Hair Color	Because you're worth it!	

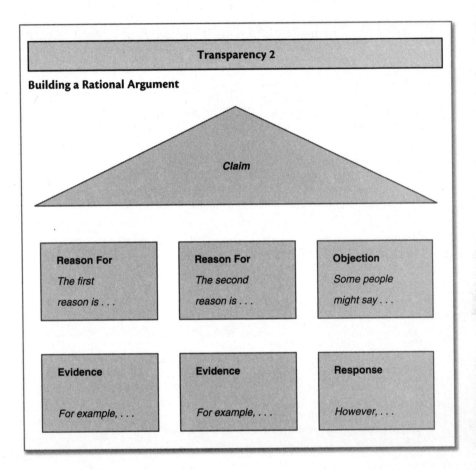

GUIDELINE #5

Encourage students to think about how almost any skill or knowledge they acquire might be used for better or for worse ends, and about how important that final end is.

When you teach, encourage students to think about how almost *any* topic they study might be used for better or worse ends, and about how important that final end is. Under the fourth guideline, we discussed how students should be encouraged to seek different solutions and to choose the one that benefits the common good rather than the individual. They should also be brought to realize that, just as there are different solutions benefiting different people, a skill or point of knowledge can be used to a good or poor end. A well-known example is that knowledge of nuclear physics can be applied to constructing bombs or to develop sources of energy, and the end to which one chooses to apply one's knowledge makes a big difference!

We are often spurred to think about how acts are put to a good or a bad end when we are faced with a dilemma, such as a situation in which we have to make a difficult choice. Everyone is faced with dilemmas, although (luckily!) most of us do not have to deal directly with dilemmas involving life and death, such as decisions to go to war, or how best to punish criminals (though in a democracy we are faced with the choice of electing the people who will deal with these dilemmas directly). Still, in our daily lives, we are often confronted with dilemmas and difficult situations in which we need to decide how to act. These everyday dilemmas still require careful consideration of multiple factors before taking an action. The step-by-step questions provided in Table 51 can help guide us and our students as we work toward solving a dilemma.

Table 51   Useful Questions to Ask Yourself When You Are Trying to Solve a Dilemma

1. Who is involved in this dilemma?
   ○ Main individual or group:
   ○ Other individuals or groups:

2. What knowledge or past experience does the main individual or group have that may help him/her or them solve this dilemma?

3. What are the interests, points of view, or deeper goals and concerns of the individual or groups involved in the situation?
   ○ Interests of main individual or group identified in question 1:
   ○ Interests of other individual or group identified in question 1:

4. What are the values or principles deemed important by the main individual or group solving the dilemma?

5. Identify the desired result that is shared by everyone involved. What is the "good" in common for all involved that the main individual or group should work toward?

6. List two or more possible and realistic responses to the dilemma.

7. Which of the responses listed above is the best response, and why?

GUIDELINE #6

Remember that a teacher is a role model!

To role-model wisdom, the teacher should adopt a Socratic approach to teaching and invite students to play a more active role in constructing learning—from their own point of view and from that of others. Wise thinking is not a set of rules or decisions that the teacher can outline for students to copy down; rather, it is a type of thinking that students themselves need to adopt and master. The most effective way to encourage wisdom-based thinking skills is not through memory drills but through student participation and teacher modeling. For example, you can capitalize on a negative event, such as two students getting into a fight, as a way to demonstrate how one can approach a similar situation in a more constructive way. The teacher can model wise thinking by saying:

> When I get into situations like this, I try to see the dispute from the perspective of the other person and think about whether, and, if so, how my own behavior might have contributed to the situation. Was there anything I could have done differently to prevent this confrontation? Is there a solution to our disagreement that is acceptable to both of us?

There are often ways of transforming what at first seems like a negative turn of events into a "teachable moment."

Also, remember never to miss an opportunity to recognize and praise good judgments made by students! For example, when a student shows consideration for others and their ideas, or when a student offers a solution that benefits the class as a whole rather than themselves as individuals, you should explicitly point out that student as an example and praise the student for displaying wise behavior. The most effective teacher is likely to be one who can create a classroom community in which wisdom is practiced rather than merely preached. Students need to understand that wisdom can and should be manifested in real life and not just on paper, and that it can lead to a more harmonious existence.

Reflection

How Can You Promote Wise Thinking in Your Classroom?

Now think about everything you have learned in this part of the book, and try to brainstorm some ideas about how you can apply it to your classroom. We are not asking you to develop a complete lesson plan or to design a curriculum, but rather, to try to apply the principles you have studied to make sure we are on the same page. You can either think of curricular activities in which you engage your students, or of ways that you can model these guidelines through your own behavior. These guidelines for teaching wisdom-based thinking skills are probably less intuitive than the principles of teaching for memory, analytical, creative, and practical skills that we discussed in previous parts of the book, and you may need to revisit sections of this part. If you are partnering up with a colleague, you may want to spend some time reflecting for yourself what each guideline means to you, and write it down below before coming together and sharing thoughts with your partner. If there is a teaching guideline for which you struggle to come up with an example, go back and read over the suggestions we offered in the text. Now it's your turn!

GUIDELINE #1

Encourage students to read classic works of literature and philosophy to learn and reflect on the wisdom of the sages.

What this guideline means to me:

_____

_____

_____

_____

Example of a curricular activity or a manner in which I can model this guideline for my students:

_____

_____

_____

_____

GUIDELINE #2

Engage students in class discussions, projects, and essays that encourage them to draw lessons from what they learn and apply these lessons to their own lives and the lives of others. Promote dialogical and dialectical thinking.

What this guideline means to me:

_____

_____

_____

_____

Example of a curricular activity or a manner in which I can model this guideline for my students:

_____

_____

_____

_____

GUIDELINE #3

Encourage students to study not only facts, but values, as developed during their reflective thinking.

What this guideline means to me:

_____

_____

_____

_____

Example of a curricular activity or a manner in which I can model this guideline for my students:

_____

_____

_____

_____

GUIDELINE #4

Place an increased emphasis on critical, creative, and practical thinking in the service of the common good.

What this guideline means to me:

_____

_____

_____

_____

Example of a curricular activity or a manner in which I can model this guideline for my students:

_____

_____

_____

_____

GUIDELINE #5

Encourage students to think about how almost any skill or knowledge they acquire might be used for better or for worse ends, and about how important that final end is.

What this guideline means to me:

_____

_____

_____

_____

Example of a curricular activity or a manner in which I can model this guideline for my students:

_____

_____

_____

_____

GUIDELINE #6

Remember that a teacher is a role model!

Think of a time when you role-modeled wise behavior to your students:

_____

_____

_____

_____

Think of a time when you did not quite know how to turn a negative event into a "teachable moment" and describe how you could have handled it differently:

_____

_____

_____

_____

PART V

Synthesis

*Helping Students Achieve
Success and Satisfaction in Their Lives*

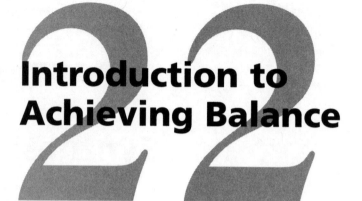

Introduction to Achieving Balance

We started out this book by briefly presenting the theoretical model of Wisdom, Intelligence, and Creativity, Synthesized (Part I). We then provided more details on how to develop classroom activities (Part II) and assessments (Part III) that address students' memory, analytical, creative, and practical skills, and showed concrete examples from different content areas and grade levels. In Part IV, we went on to discuss the importance of showing students how to apply their skills and knowledge toward a common good, and described some general principles of teaching for wisdom.

In this concluding section, we will summarize the main topics discussed in the book by reviewing how to balance the different thinking skills in the activities and assignments you choose for your classroom. You will find further examples of balanced lesson plans for different grade levels and in different subject areas, and you will be provided with templates that you can use to develop your own enhanced lesson plans and assessments.

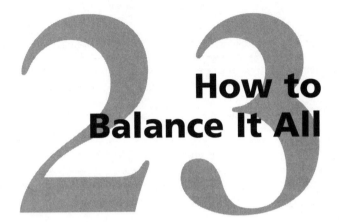

How to Balance It All

To teach for Wisdom, Intelligence, and Creativity, Synthesized (WICS) is to create a supportive learning environment in which students find their own ability patterns within or across academic domains, understand how uniqueness allows each individual to make a particular contribution to the learning community, and value diversity. One step toward this goal is to *balance* the types of activities you offer your students so as to broaden the range of abilities addressed and to give more students a chance to capitalize on their strengths (and compensate for their weaknesses).

To achieve this balance, it can be helpful to have a chart that allows you to see, in one glance, which types of thinking skills you are addressing in your lesson or your curriculum unit (e.g., a sequence of lessons). In Tables 52–55, you will find examples of such overview charts from curriculum units that we have created. You will see that we have used slightly different formats, depending on what is important for each specific unit. For example, for the science unit described in Table 52, it was important to have a balance between different thinking skills in each lesson, whereas in the art unit described in Table 53, we were more concerned about an overall balance throughout the unit while paying attention to providing both group and individual activities. In the math unit described in Table 55, in contrast, the main concern was to promote vocabulary growth in students in addition to enhancing their comprehension of the mathematical concepts being taught. As a rule of thumb, you should always try to balance the thinking skills you address (memory, analytical, creative, and practical) in order to address a broader range of learners, but feel free to take into account other parameters as they matter most to the specific class that you are teaching.

Table 52 Balancing Analytical, Creative, and Practical Activities in an Elementary/Middle School Science Unit on Light

Lessons	Analytical	Creative	Practical
"Straight From the Sun"	Interpret observational data.	Create new transparent and translucent objects by combining as many materials as possible.	Plan and construct a scoring sheet to enable judges to fairly judge translucent and transparent objects.
"Exploring Mirrors"	Make and verify predictions.	Design a mirror Exploratorium. * Design a mirror maze.	Use mirrors to direct light around corners. * Build a kaleidoscope. * Build a periscope.
"Can You Bend a Pencil Without Breaking It?"	Compare and contrast observational data and draw conclusions.	Use refraction as a clue in a mystery. * Write the memoirs of a light beam, *One Week on Earth: A Light Beam's Story.*	Use knowledge of refraction to improve one's ability to catch a fish in an aquarium.
"The Power of the Lens"	Compare and contrast different lenses.	Write a conversation that might take place between a person who wears convex lenses and a person who wears concave lenses in a game situation.	Build an exhibit showing the different uses of lenses.
"Creating Rainbows"	Compare and contrast colors of a prism and colors of the rainbow.	Explore ways light can be separated into different colors using different objects and how the process could be reversed. Write a story in which the characteristics of light play a major role.	Select one idea from the creative activity and design an experiment to test the idea.
"Where Did All the Colors Go?"	Make and verify predictions about color filters.	Create a cartoon strip illustrating the key concepts learned in this unit. * Create a colorful stained glass window using three colored filters—red, blue, and green. * Create a cartoon strip illustrating the key concepts learned in this unit.	* Design an experiment to explain differences in the intensity of the color. * Write and illustrate a book in which students explain how to make toys using their knowledge of light. * Make sample toys for a book on light.

*Denotes an optional activity.

Table 53 Balancing Analytical, Creative, and Practical Activities in a High School Art Unit on the Nineteenth Century Impressionist Movement

Summary of activities during this unit:

Type of activity	Creative	Analytical/Memory	Practical
Individual	Make a sketch or a drawing.	Fill out the vocabulary worksheet.	Convince a friend of your knowledge.
Group	Pretend to be an art critic in Paris in 1876.	Analyze an Impressionist painting.	Do color-mixes.
Assessments	Sketch or drawing.	Vocabulary test.	Writing assignment.

Detailed description of select activities:

Analytical. Analyze an Impressionist painting. Divide the class into groups of three or four. Give each group a postcard representing an Impressionist painting and a postcard representing a "classical" (pre-Impressionist) painting. Ask students to compare and contrast the two paintings. In what way is the Impressionist painting different from the "classical" art form? Referring to the text that the class has read about Impressionism, the important elements for the comparison are: theme, light, color, contours, use of brush strokes, and perspective. Then have one member of the group present the results to the rest of the class. Ask the students to include the five new vocabulary words in their description (*attenuate, ephemeral, iridescent, obscure,* and *predominate*). Make sure to prompt them during their presentation if they forget to use the new words.

Creative. Divide the class into groups of three or four. Ask each group to imagine that they, like Albert Wolff, are art critics in Paris in 1876. Ask them to think of a description of this new painting style, either a positive or a negative one, depending on how they themselves feel. The important thing to remember is that they should imagine they are in 1876, so they cannot make reference to anything that has happened after that time period. Then have one member of the group present the results to the rest of the class.

Practical. You have now read the whole introduction to Impressionism and have seen examples of Impressionist painters. Imagine you are visiting a museum with a friend, and want to "show off" your great knowledge of Impressionism. What would you tell your friend to impress him or her with your knowledge? You can imagine that you are standing in front of a painting and may write your answer in dialogue form. Feel free to express your opinion about Impressionism.

Table 54   Balancing Analytical, Creative, and Practical Activities in an Elementary School Language Arts Unit on the Biography Genre

Lessons	Analytical Activities	Creative Activities	Practical Activities
Lesson 1 (1 day) "Introduction to Biography as Genre"	Identify life facts. * Sort life facts.	Come up with a title for your own biography.	Write biographical statements about friends/family members.
Lesson 2 (1 day) "Vocabulary: Compound Words from Greek Roots"	Identify roots in compound words.	Create a mini-dictionary of coined compound words.	Find examples in texts and media and begin a scrapbook.
Lesson 3 (1 day) "Chronology"	Sequence "photos" in chronological order.	Create a captioned, dated photo to precede and follow other photos.	Sequence school day events. Sequence class members by dates of birth. Add chronology examples to scrapbook.
Lesson 4 (1 day) "Descriptive Vocabulary"	Preview reading by title and photos. Practice vocabulary.	Create a picture of Lincoln, captioned with descriptive vocabulary.	Identify friends and TV characters fitting descriptions.
Lesson 5 (1 day) "Reading *The Mysterious Mr. Lincoln* in Freedman's (1987) *Lincoln: A Photobiography*"	Preview chapter by title. Practice guided reading. Review cloze passages.	Illustrate an idiom; write to Lincoln (also a variety of optional activities).	Describe friends and TV characters (also a variety of optional activities).
Lesson 6 (1 day) "Vocabulary: Reading More About Mr. Lincoln"	Practice vocabulary. Learn cloze and inference activities.	Invent creative comparisons.	Find new vocabulary in reading a passage.

*Denotes an optional activity.

Table 55 Balancing Analytical, Creative, and Practical Activities in a High School Mathematics Unit on the Properties of Exponents

Summary of activities during this unit:

Lessons	Creative	Analytical/Memory	Practical
Vocabulary	Invent new names.	Write definitions.	Think of examples of prime and composite numbers. Apply scientific notation to real-world situations.
Comprehension	Imagine large numbers as the characters of a TV show.	Complete exercises with the first three properties of exponents. Explain the advantages of using a base system.	Express daily behavior using scientific notations. Complete cube coloring problem. Explain properties of exponents.

Detailed descriptions of select activities:

Analytical. Why is it convenient to use a base system? Explain the main advantage of this system in one or two sentences.

Creative. Just what is the base system? Instead of counting and naming endless strings of units, we count in bundles or sets. A numerical base is the number of units in a bundle. Within a given base, the bundles of each order all have the same number of units. The most common base is the one we employ in the West today: the decimal base, or base ten. In the base ten system we name digits one through nine, plus zero, to form the first-order bundle. After nine we reuse the names in different forms to indicate the second order, or power (the teens), the third power (the twenties), etc. Come up with new names for the first nine digits.

Practical. Cube coloring problem: In groups of three or four, use the sixteen cubes (distributed by teacher and to be assembled with glue or tape). A single cube is the cube on its first birthday, when it has eight corners, and six faces. Your group task is to build a cube on its second birthday and describe it in terms of the number of corners and faces. Continue to explore the cube on its third, fourth, etc., birthday. On its tenth birthday, the cube is dipped into a bucket of paint. Take it apart into unit cubes: How many unit cubes are painted on (1) three faces, (2) two faces, and (3) one face, respectively?

At this point you may be wondering, "How aware should my students be of this balanced approach to teaching?" We fully encourage you to share with students that you are proposing a range of activities that will address the different strengths of students in your classroom. This knowledge will help to increase students' metacognition, or awareness, and ability to consider their own thinking processes. That is, students should learn about the different kinds of thinking required for participation in analytical, practical, and creative learning experiences. Some teachers with whom we have worked post "thinking verbs" (see Table 56) in their classrooms. In this way, the teachers remind students about analytical, creative, practical, and wise thinking skills.

Although some students may demonstrate strength in one particular kind of thinking, all students will benefit from processing content in all three ways. If explicitly taught how to think analytically, creatively, and practically, students will become more comfortable with all three ways of thinking. If students are asked to think aloud in their strong modality, other students will benefit from the cognitive modeling. By designing a proportional number of analytical, creative, and practical activities you

Table 56   Thinking Verbs

Mnemonic	Analytical	Creative	Practical
Recall	Analyze	Imagine	Apply
Name	Compare	Invent	Use
Retell	Contrast	Suppose	Implement
Say	Evaluate	Design	Do
Recite	Explain	Create	Connect to real life
Describe	Critique	Brainstorm	Find examples in
List	Organize	Restructure	Real life
Identify	Sort	Synthesize	Translate
Locate	Classify	Combine	Demonstrate
Match	Sequence	Predict	Utilize

To be wise is to:

Apply your intelligence, creativity, and knowledge toward the achievement of a common good.

Consider your own point of view and interests as well as the point of view and interests of people around you and of your community as a whole.

Take into account short- as well as long-term consequences of your actions.

Engage in reflective, dialectical, and dialogical thinking.

will ensure that all students have opportunities to participate in all three types of tasks. This is important because students need opportunities not only to capitalize on their strengths but also to expand their cognitive repertoires.

To encourage all students to enhance their thinking skills in a broad range of domains, it is also important to assess students in different domains. Tables 57 and 58 provide examples of how assignments and assessments around a core concept (i.e., number sense in the math example in Table 57, or experimental design in the psychology example in Table 58) can tap into different thinking skills.

Table 57 Analytical, Practical, and Creative Items From an Elementary School Homework Assignment in Mathematics on Number Sense

---

Analytical Item

The numbers 41 and 14 both have the digit "4" and the digit "1." Explain how the numbers are different using place value.

Practical Item

You have ten bills in your wallet or purse. You have a total of $343. How many $1, $10, and $100 bills might you have? (Hint: Think of your Base Ten blocks!)

Creative Item

Pretend you are building a house using only the following Base Ten blocks:

Ones blocks look like this   Tens blocks look like this

Hundreds blocks look like this

Design a house that uses exactly 343 blocks. Remember a ones block equals 1 block, a tens block equals 10 blocks, and a hundreds block equals 100 blocks. Figure out how many of each type of block you will use.

How many ones blocks? _____   Tens blocks? _____
Hundreds blocks? _____

Draw the house using the correct number of each type of block.

Table 58   Analytical, Practical, and Creative Items From a High School Assessment in Psychology (A.P. Level)

Assessment Questions:

Stem. A variety of research methods are used in psychology.

a. What is a quasi-experimental design?

b. A researcher devises a test to predict success in elementary-school mathematics. The test requires students to do simple arithmetic word problems. As predicted, the researcher finds that her test predicts mathematics grades. The correlation is an impressive .55. She therefore labels her test the Sure-Fire Mathematics Abilities Test. She describes her test as measuring the "fundamental abilities causal of success in school mathematics." What are the potential errors in her claims?

c. What do you believe to be a fundamental ability involved in high performance in mathematics at the fifth-grade (elementary school) level? Design a study to test your hypothesis.

d. When schools give standardized ability tests, a number of factors at the time of testing can contribute to scores being either higher or lower than they should be. What would be two examples each of such factors that might erroneously lead to (a) higher scores and (b) lower scores?

Scoring Rubric:

Question A [Memory]: 1 point for noting the idea that groups are not randomly assigned.

Question B [Analytical]: 1 point for each of the possible explanations listed below:

- The test is not so much an ability test as it is an achievement test. It measures skills taught in elementary school mathematics. It therefore should be relabeled as an achievement test.

- The correlation of .55 is not high enough to draw any kind of causal conclusion.

- The researcher cannot conclude that, whatever her test measures, it is causal. Scores on it may be a result of success in school mathematics or both test and school success may be dependent on one or more higher order variables.

- The test certainly does not measure all the aptitudes needed for success in school mathematics. Other mathematics skills and other skills (such as reading) are also required.

Question C [Creative]: 1 point for describing what they believe is a fundamental ability (e.g., working memory); 2 points for the quality of their study design (e.g., experimental design with control groups and random assignment; discussion of the relevant sample such as the bottom third compared to the top third of the students in the class; control for extraneous variables such as IQ).

Question D [Practical]: 2 points for listing two factors associated with higher scores (e.g., cheating, being given extra time); 2 points for listing two factors associated with lower scores (e.g., environmental factors such as poor lighting, uncomfortable chairs, and distracting noises at the time of the test). Note that if they list two factors, but do not indicate which direction they could impact (positive or negative), they should only receive 2 points.

A Word of Wisdom on Learning Goals

A final word of wisdom when it comes to lesson planning and curriculum design: it is important to ensure that all the analytical, creative, practical, and wisdom-based learning experiences encourage students to learn the content. In our work, we have found that teachers draw on their own creative strengths to design activities that appeal to the students they teach. In creating new activities, teachers often start with ideas taken from the content they teach. For example, if students are reading a mystery in which detectives are trying to break a secret code, teachers may borrow the idea to develop activities in which students translate a secret code (analytical activity), invent a secret code (creative activity), or think of everyday applications in which codes might be useful, such as PINs at ATM machines (practical activity).

These activities in themselves, however, are only loosely connected to the content (as the source of the idea). Because these activities do not explicitly guide students to master particular language arts skills, students may think they are learning how to invent and crack codes, rather than understanding the underlying task of learning about mysteries or other language arts concepts. It is important, therefore, to consider curriculum objectives when designing the activities. For example, if the curriculum requires students to learn certain vocabulary or spelling words related to reading a mystery (e.g., *detective, red herring*), you might ask students to invent (creative activity) a code to encode the vocabulary words, which students might next exchange with classmates who would then "crack the code" (analytical activity). In this case, the creative and analytical activities have been designed to promote the acquisition of the target content (i.e., the vocabulary of mystery). You must guide your students to understand that the purpose of the activity is not to learn how to devise or decipher codes but rather to learn the language arts content. Following this instructional design principle will ensure that analytical/creative/practical instruction is not an "add-on" but rather an integral part of the curriculum.

In sum, there are four general principles that should guide curriculum development for analytical/creative/practical instruction. In any given unit, you should (1) maintain a balance of analytical, creative, and practical instruction; (2) teach students how to think analytically, creatively, and practically; (3) design analytical/creative/practical learning experiences that help students learn the content instead of designing such experiences as "add-ons"; and (4) verify that students have achieved the learning goals through a blend of assessments that tap into different thinking skills. Table 59 provides a summary of the major steps involved in successful lesson and curriculum planning that we have discussed in this book.

Table 59 Summary of Steps to Follow in Designing a Lesson Plan or Unit

1. *Determine the content to be taught.* What is the content that I need to teach in this lesson or this unit?

2. *Define objectives.* What do students have to learn (both knowledge and skills)? What do I want students to learn? What do students want to learn? Spell out the overarching learning objective of your lesson or unit and the specific learning goals that you want students to achieve.

3. *Specify a time line.* Within what time frame do I want these goals to be accomplished? Divide the unit into lessons (if you are preparing a full unit) and structure the lessons by type: explanation/discovery, practice, students' self-study, assessment. How many lessons can I spend on this unit? How do I want to structure this unit? Will the unit include lectures? Will the unit include group activities? Will the unit include homework? What kinds of assessment (if any) will the unit include?

4. *Determine which learning channels are most suitable for which components of the content.* Generate a list of analytical, creative, and practical activities that span the content of the unit.

(Continued)

(Continued)

5. *Decide how to incorporate the learning channels into the transmission of the material.* Sequence analytical, creative, and practical activities. Consider logical sequence, lesson flow, and the dynamics of learning. Balance the unit using a variety of lesson elements.

6. *Design matching assessments.* Use various types of assessment to measure student learning. Follow the three steps described in the section devoted to assessment: (1) identify the most important learning goals to be assessed, (2) determine which ability levels should be assessed, and (3) design a balanced set of assessment questions tapping into different cognitive skills (e.g., memory, analytical, creative, and practical) and using different item formats (e.g., forced choice, open-ended, performance based). Don't forget to develop a rubric for scoring your open-ended assessment items!

25 Wisdom, Intelligence, and Creativity, Synthesized

In the very first part and chapter of this book we gave you a brief overview of the theoretical model of human cognition (thinking and learning) that guides our approach to teaching and assessment. This model is referred to as the WICS model because it states that, in order to function successfully in society, one needs to display wisdom, intelligence, and creativity. These characteristics need to be balanced into an integrated synthesis.

Throughout the sections of this book, we have tried to illustrate how a theory of cognition can be translated into effective classroom practices, by showing you how to model wisdom (Part IV), how to design and engage your students in a balance of memory, analytical, creative, and practical learning experiences (Part II), how to assess for these different skills (Part III), and, finally, how to balance it all (this section, Part V). We hope that these illustrations have given you a clear idea of how you can expand your teaching repertoire to enhance learning for a broad range of students in your classroom, and that you will apply these suggestions in your own lesson planning.

Tables 60 and 61 can be used as templates to guide your own lesson or unit planning, and Table 62 can be used as a checklist for reviewing lesson plans you have developed previously, or to examine the balance of your textbook's activities. When designing your own curriculum, keep in mind the different steps involved in setting learning objectives and balancing activities summarized in Table 59. Most important though, remember that designing a lesson plan is a rewarding and enjoyable activity. See what a pleasure it is for all your students to succeed with their individual profiles of strengths and weaknesses.

Table 60 Template A for Lesson Design

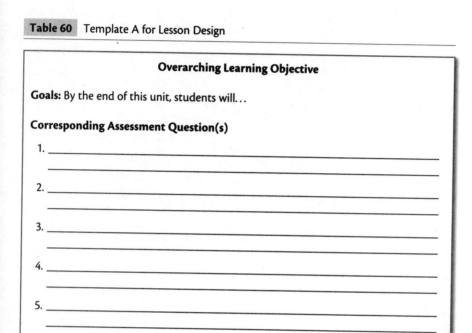

Overarching Learning Objective

Goals: By the end of this unit, students will. . .

Corresponding Assessment Question(s)

1. _____

_____

2. _____

_____

3. _____

_____

4. _____

_____

5. _____

_____

	Memory	More Analytical	More Practical	More Creative
Multiple-Choice				
Open-Ended				
Performance/Product				

Table 61   Template B for Lesson Design

Learning Objective

Goals: By the end of this unit, students will...

1. _____

2. _____

3. _____

4. _____

5. _____

Essential Questions:

Mostly Creative	Mostly Analytical	Mostly Practical

District/State Goals and Objectives:

Materials Needed:

Table 62 Sample Checklist to Review Lesson or Textbook Content for Balance and Standards Met

Activity description	Activity is mostly	Learning goal or state or district standard met by this activity
	❑ C ❑ A ❑ P ❑ M	
	❑ C ❑ A ❑ P ❑ M	
	❑ C ❑ A ❑ P ❑ M	
	❑ C ❑ A ❑ P ❑ M	

Answer Key

CHAPTER 5

How could you remember all twenty digits next time? One key to memorization is organization. If you look at this string of numbers (11231302928527246060), you will see that it's not a random sample of digits, but that one can find a logical pattern: In **1** year there are **12** months, comprising **31**, **30**, **29**, or **28** days, and these days are divided into **52** weeks, each week comprising **7** days made up of **24** hours divided into **60** minutes each hour, and **60** seconds each minute.

Let's try again. Can you remember this string of digits?

39152127

Now think of the multiplication table for the number 3; keep only odd multipliers. . . .

CHAPTER 9

Activity	Main Skill	Rationale
Psychology	Practical	In this activity you are asking students to relate knowledge to their own lives. Of course it requires some analytical and memory skills (they must first understand and then remember what "peer pressure" means); it is primarily a practical activity.
Statistics	Creative	In this activity you are asking students to use data in a creative way. Of course it requires some analytical skills to understand how the data can be tweaked for new uses and some practical skills to figure out how you will relate to other people and convince them of your message, but it is primarily a creative activity because students are asked to come up with novel ideas.
Geography	Memory	You may have thought this was an analytical activity because the instructions contain the words "compare and contrast" and "categorize," but it is really more of a recognition memory task in which you do not have to analyze any attributes of the countries, just recognize the initial letter of their name.
Literature	Analytical	In this activity you ask students to analyze the text for temporal keys and then explain how these keys are used, so it is a high-level analytical task.
Physical Education	Memory	In this activity you ask students to memorize rules (not necessarily to understand them!).
Biology	All of the above	This was a bit of a trick question, because it is a complex activity that really involves all cognitive skills. You need analytical skills to research information about the creature and evaluate which facts will be pertinent to argue your case; you need memory to remember these facts in the heat of your presentation; you need practical skills to come up with arguments that will convince others of your point of view; and you need to be creative to imagine yourself as a gobi, a seahorse, or a clownfish!

Appendix to Part I

Suggested Further Readings

Below are suggested further readings for those who want to learn more about the Wisdom, Intelligence, and Creativity, Synthesized (WICS) model and other resources on teaching strategies.

In the introductory section of this book, we offered a brief overview of the WICS model. After reading the summary, some of you may still say to yourself something like: "This all sounds very nice, but how does it actually work in the classroom?" In this Appendix to Part I, we provide references for some articles illustrating how we have gone about evaluating to the effectiveness of teaching students based on the WICS model, as compared with not addressing the WICS skills in the curriculum. We will also provide references to other authors' work.

REFERENCES FOR FURTHER READINGS FROM THE PACE CENTER

- Sternberg, R. J., Ferrari, M., Clinkenbeard, R. P., & Grigorenko, E. L. (1996). Identification, instruction, and assessment of gifted children: A construct validation of a triarchic model. *Gifted Child Quarterly, 40,* 129–137.

In this study, Sternberg and colleagues offered a summer program to high school students in which they matched students' learning styles with the type of teaching they received, to see if students would learn better if they were taught at least some of the time in a way that enabled them to capitalize on their strengths. The motivation for the study was to show that conventional means of teaching and assessment may systematically undervalue the learning potentials of creatively and practically oriented students. These students may have the ability to perform quite well, but may achieve at lower levels than they are capable of because neither the form of instruction nor the form of assessment properly matches their pattern of strength. The authors found that students who were better matched in terms of their pattern of abilities outperformed students who were more poorly matched. This study is important because it shows that when students' learning styles are addressed in the teaching they receive, they perform better. In most regular classrooms, however, it is not realistic to assess each individual student and to individualize the teaching. Teachers have to deal with a group of diverse students with different learning needs. The best way to reach all students then becomes broadening the teaching repertoire and offering all students a balance of memory, analytical, practical, and creative activities. This is what occurred in the next illustration.

- Sternberg, R. J., Torff, B., & Grigorenko, E. L. (1998). Teaching for successful intelligence raises school achievement. *Phi Delta Kappa, 79*, 667–669.

This article reports two studies conducted with third and eighth graders. Sternberg and colleagues showed that instruction that combines memory, analytical, practical, and creative activities is superior to other forms of instruction, regardless of students' ability patterns. Such balanced instruction helps students both to capitalize on their strengths and to remediate and compensate for their weaknesses. In the elementary school study, students also were administered a self-assessment questionnaire in which they were asked how much they had liked the curriculum, how much they thought they had learned with the curriculum, and how well they thought they had performed with the curriculum. The students in the group that received a balanced memory, analytical, practical, creative curriculum generally gave significantly higher ratings than did the students in the other two groups, who received more typical curricula.

- Sternberg, R. J., Grigorenko, E. L., & Jarvin, L. (2001). Improving reading instruction: The triarchic model. *Educational Leadership, 58* (6), 48–52.

This article reports on three studies that were conducted at the middle and high school levels, with a shared focus on enhancing students' reading comprehension. As in earlier studies, the research team attempted to help teachers do better what they were already doing (i.e., teaching reading), rather than giving them a new curriculum. The goal was to supplement standard reading instruction—which included both phonic and whole-language elements—with a specific intervention balancing memory, analytical, practical, and creative skills. Teachers in the control condition were shown how to apply mnemonic strategies. Overall, the analyses showed a distinct advantage of the intervention group over the memory-based control group.

- Grigorenko, E. L., Jarvin, L., & Sternberg, R. J. (2002). School-based tests of the triarchic theory of human intelligence: Three settings, three samples, three syllabi. *Contemporary Educational Psychology, 27,* 167–208.

This article focuses on the same middle and high school studies of reading comprehension described above, but provides much more detail on the evaluation and statistical methods used to analyze the data collected.

- Sternberg, R. J., & Grigorenko, E. L. (2007). *Teaching for Successful Intelligence* (2nd ed.). Thousand Oaks, CA: Corwin Press.

This book contains further examples of classroom activities and curricula.

REFERENCES TO OTHER AUTHORS' WORK

Although the examples in this book all come from the PACE Center's work, there are many authors who have studied and written about teaching strategies and best ways to foster both analytical and creative skills in students. Below are more suggested further readings, starting with the classic works on curriculum development and ending with the most recent research-based suggestions for instruction.

There are hundreds of books on curriculum development and curriculum reform, but three of the classics are Ralph W. Tyler's 1949 *Basic Principles of Curriculum & Instruction,* printed in paperback by the University of Chicago Press in 1969 and still available today; Hilda Taba's 1962 *Curriculum Development: Theory and Practice,* issued by Harcourt Publishing; and Elliot W. Eisner's *Reimagining Schools: The Selected Works of Elliot W. Eisner,* a summary of decades of his works published by Routledge in 2005. In addition to these seminal works by the authors, there are many books available *about* Tyler, Taba, or Eisner, just to name those. Your librarian or bookstore will be able to guide you through the wealth of resources available on curriculum development, from the more theoretical treatises to the hands-on guides.

When it comes to learning theory and how it applies to instruction and assessment, the big classic is Benjamin S. Bloom's 1956 *Taxonomy of Educational Objectives, Handbook 1: Cognitive Domain* published by Longman, which nearly all (if not all) students of education will have heard of, although many will be more familiar with his work through reading about it rather than the book itself. Use any search engine on the Web and you will find hundreds of websites that discuss Bloom's taxonomy! His taxonomy has recently been revised by one of his former collaborators, Lori W. Anderson, and a colleague of hers, David R. Krathwohl in *A Taxonomy for Learning, Teaching, and Assessing: A Revision of Bloom's Taxonomy of Educational Objectives* (2000), and this is poised to become the new reference. A more recent reference, who in many circles is as well-known to educators as Bloom, is Howard Gardner and his theory of Multiple Intelligences. The theory is most recently described in *Multiple Intelligences: New Horizons*, published by Perseus in 2006, and he has also written numerous books on other topics related to education, such as the role of creativity, which he discussed in the 1994 volume *Creating Minds: An Anatomy of Creativity seen through the lives of Freud, Einstein, Picasso, Stravinsky, Eliot, Graham, and Gandhi*. The number of additional authors having thought and written about learning theory are too many to mention here, and if we were to try we would necessarily miss out on many important names. An education or psychology textbook might be a good place to start learning more about this broad field.

Finally, there is an increasing interest in research-based instructional methods, and we are in no way trying to claim that we are the only ones supporting our suggestions with empirical evidence. The Association for Supervision and Curriculum Development (ASCD) publishes both journals and books on research-based instruction, such as *Classroom Instruction That Works: Research-Based Strategies for Increasing Student Achievement*, by R. J. Marzano, D. J. Pickering, and J. F. Pollock (2004). Another good starting place for finding more resources on research-based instruction is the Department of Education Institute for Education Science (IES) online clearinghouse called *What Works*, see http://ies.ed.gov/ncee/wwc/.

Appendix to Part II

Mnemonic Techniques and Strategies

THE METHOD OF LOCI

The method known as loci is one of the oldest mnemonic techniques known and has been used since antiquity. Roman and Greek orators were able to memorize long speeches by dividing the speech into chunks of thought and associating each thought of a speech to a place in their home (*loci* is Latin for *places*). In the method of loci, each thought is associated to a place in your house (or any other location you know well), so that when you mentally walk through the house, the thoughts come back to you. For example, the opening thought of a speech would be associated to the front door, the second thought to the entryway, the third to a piece of furniture in the entryway, and so on. When the orator wanted to remember his or her speech, thought by thought, he or she took a mental tour through his or her own home. Thinking of the front door reminded the orator of the first thought of the speech, the second "place" (the entryway) of the second thought, and so on to the end of the speech.

Here is an illustration of the method taken from a math lesson on fractions. The same idea can be applied to any piece of information, be it in mathematics, language arts, science, social studies, or another subject area.

---

1. Make large size representations for each of the three fractions 1/2, 2/4, and 4/8. Ensure that the fractions are of an adequate size so that students can clearly read them from anywhere in the classroom.

(Continued)

(Continued)

2. Choose three locations in your classroom that are clearly visible to students. Ensure that the three locations are equivalent to each other. For example, choose three windows or three bulletin boards or three walls of your class. These locations will be used to tape or pin each of the three fractions 1/2, 2/4, and 4/8 at one of each of these three locations. The locations must be equivalent to each other, just as the fractions are equivalent to each other.

3. Hold up the 1/2 and 2/4 fraction cards. Have the students repeat together the names of the fractions. Have them repeat together that 1/2 = 2/4 and that 2/4 = 1/2.

   "What's the name of this fraction? (1/2) What is it equivalent to?" (2/4) "What is the name of this fraction? (2/4) What is it equivalent to?" (1/2)

4. Students should recognize 1/2 = 2/4 = 4/8. Have them repeat together the names of the fractions and the equivalencies.

5. Tape or pin each of the fractions to the three equivalent locations in your classroom. Point out to students that you are placing them in equivalent locations to show that they are equivalent fractions. Have the students close their eyes and tell you what fraction is in each location (e.g., if you have placed the fractions on three windows of your class, ask them, "What fraction is on the window at the front? What fraction is on the middle window? What fraction is on the back window?"). Ask them to look at the fraction and then close their eyes and visualize each fraction on the window. Ask them to repeat back to you why you have placed these three fractions all on windows or all on bulletin boards, etc.

THE PEG SYSTEM

The principle underlying the peg system is to "peg" new facts to be remembered to a known sequence of cues. Since the cues (the pegs) are a well-known sequence, there is little risk of forgetting or leaving out a piece of information—gaps will be immediately obvious.

The peg number system is an easy technique for remembering lists of items in a specific order. This technique helps you build up pictures in your mind, in which the numbers are represented by things that rhyme with the number, and are linked to images that represent the things to be remembered. First you have to associate each number between one and ten with a word that can be pictured. You can pick any word you like, but it is preferable that the word rhymes with, or is linked to, the number in some other fashion. For example, you can use the following words:

1. Gum

2. Shoe

3. Tree

4. Floor

5. Hive

6. Sticks

7. Heaven

8. Gate

9. Line

10. Hen

Once you have established a firm link between the numbers and a word, you can use that word to link the new knowledge. For example, you can use the following list to remember the first ten U.S. presidents, or the sequence of experiments to be recalled for a science exam.

Ask students to work in groups of two or three and to memorize this list of the first ten American presidents using the peg-word list above:

1. George Washington (for example, Washington loved to chew **gum.** To retrieve the information, say to yourself: **One** is for **gum**—who likes to chew gum? It was **Washington**. So, Washington is one.)

2. John Adams (for example, Adams always had holes in his **shoes**)

Your turn:

3. Thomas Jefferson: _____

4. James Madison: _____

5. James Monroe: _____

6. John Quincy Adams: _____

7. Andrew Jackson: _____

8. Martin van Buren: _____

9. William Henry Harrison: _____

10. John Tyler: _____

ACRONYMS AND ACROSTICS

An acronym is a word formed by the initial letters of a string of words. For example, USA stands for United States of America. Another acronym is HOMES, a help to remember the names of the great lakes: *H*uron *O*ntario *M*ichigan *E*rie *S*uperior.

Can you think of other acronyms that you use in the classroom? Write them down here:

_____

_____

_____

An acrostic is a phrase or a verse in which the first letters form the word or information you want to remember. The following example can be used in the mathematics or science classroom.

Tell the students that there is a process for conducting a study. It is called the "inquiry process." The inquiry process has six steps.

1. Ask the question.

2. Predict your results.

3. Investigate.

4. Analyze.

5. Graph and table.

6. Explain.

Explain that sometimes it is difficult to remember all the steps and that you are going to give students a trick to help them remember. Ask them to write the first letter of each step on a page. Tell them the mnemonic for the process is:
*A*lways *P*repare *I*ntensely *A*nd *G*et *E*xcellent, for example.
Now come up with your own: _____
Then ask the students to close their eyes and picture someone preparing intensely for a test and then getting excellent results, or ask them to draw a picture. Then show students how remembering this sentence will give them the first letter in each step of the inquiry process.

Can you think of other acrostics that you use in the classroom? Write them down here:

_____

_____

_____

THE LINK METHOD: INCORPORATING THE INFORMATION TO BE REMEMBERED IN A STORY

The principle underlying the link method is to make associations between items in a list, for example by linking them in a story. Three "tricks" will make this strategy even more effective:

Substitute by picturing one item instead of another.

Exaggerate and turn the information you need to remember into something ridiculous.

Put some *Action* in the story you're creating.

Here is an example of how you can remember information by linking the different pieces of information in a story.

Imagine that you have to memorize the list of the first ten U.S. states in alphabetical order.

1. Alabama
2. Alaska
3. Arizona
4. Arkansas
5. California
6. Colorado
7. Connecticut
8. Delaware
9. Florida
10. Georgia

(Continued)

(Continued)

First, think of a substitute word that reminds you of the name of each state. For example, *Alabama* might remind you of *sweet home*, from the song "Sweet Home Alabama," so you can substitute Alabama with the image of a home, because a home is easier to picture than Alabama. For *Alaska*, you can picture a wild salmon or a bear. Then you link the two images together: picture a family of salmons living in a home, or saying "home sweet home."

Now think of a story that links together all ten states:

_____

_____

_____

A slightly different version of the link system is to put the information to be remembered in a poem that rhymes. The following example is taken from a mathematics lesson on the concept of average.

As you demonstrate examples of what an average is, teach the students the following rhyme to help them remember.

When an average you must find
Don't you worry. Don't you mind.
First add up all the numbers in the set.
Then write down the total that you get.
Then count up all the numbers and divide
By the number of numbers that you find.

GRAPHIC AIDS AND ORGANIZERS

Graphic aids can be used both to organize the information to encode it more efficiently and to help retrieve the information.

A Know-Want to Know-Learned (KWL) chart is a powerful way to organize information in a way that makes it easier to remember. The following example is taken from a lesson on Abraham Lincoln, but the same principle can be applied in any subject matter area.

Use the KWL strategy to help students organize information while they read and then to retrieve it. KWL stands for:

- what you already KNOW before reading
- what you will WANT to know (look for) during reading
- what you have LEARNED after reading

Review what a biography is and what types of information students are likely to find when they read the story of someone's life. Review the life fact categories on the KWL chart. Then ask the students what life facts they remember about President Abraham Lincoln. As students volunteer what they remember, write the "life facts" in the appropriate category row. The chart should look something like this:

Facts	What I Know	What I Want to Know	What I Learned
List by categories (e.g., a story or a character's appearance).	Abe was tall and lean. He wore a stovepipe hat. He had long, bony legs.	Did he look young or old? Did he have a beard?	Complete as you read the story.

Another way to use graphic and visual aids to remember information is to play the memory game, in which a word or a fact is associated with a picture. Here is an example from a vocabulary lesson, but the same principle can be applied to any other kind of material.

The Memory Game

Prepare a set of word and picture cards. Tape them to the wall, face down, in random order. Once the cards are taped, face down, it is helpful to number the backs of the cards.

Tell the students that they will be playing a game to improve their memory and concentration. The object of the game is to remember where the words and matching pictures are. Ask one student to call out any two numbers. Turn those numbered cards face up and check to see if they match. Make sure everyone can

(Continued)

(Continued)

see what the cards say. Encourage the class to remember where those cards are. Then turn them back, face down, and go on to the next student, who will call out two more numbers. Proceed in this way until someone turns up a card that "matches" one that has already been called out. Encourage the player to remember where the card's "match" was. Whenever a student calls out two numbers whose cards "match," that student scores a point and gets another turn. Then remove the matched cards from the board. The matched cards can be given to the students to keep score. The student with the most matched pairs wins.

After you have sufficiently modeled the memory game, pair students and give each pair a set of vocabulary word and picture cards to arrange face down on a table. Have them play the memory game with their partners.

Appendix to Part III

Cross-Reference of Sample Tables

Below is a cross-reference of sample tables arranged by grade level, content area, response format (MC for multiple-choice or OE for open-ended), and cognitive skill type assessed.

			Memory	Analytical	Creative	Practical
Elementary and Middle School	Math	MC	Table 33			
		OE				
	Language Arts	MC				
		OE			Table 38	Table 45
	Science	MC				
		OE		Table 36	Table 39	Table 46
High School	Math	MC				
		OE		Table 37	Table 40	Table 47
	Language Arts	MC				
		OE				
	Science	MC				
		OE	Table 32			

See any blank cells? First go through the text and find examples that were not in tables to complete the grid. Then use your imagination and come up with assessment questions to complete any blank cells!

References

Anderson, L. W., Krathwohl, D. R., & Bloom, B. S. (2000). *A taxonomy for learning, teaching, and assessing: A revision of Bloom's taxonomy of educational objectives.* New York: Longman.

Bloom, B. S. (1956). *Taxonomy of educational objectives, handbook 1: Cognitive domain.* New York: Longman.

Eisner, E. W. (2005). *Reimagining schools: The selected works of Elliot W. Eisner.* New York: Routledge.

Franklin, B. (1988). *Poor Richard's almanac* (Rev. ed.). White Plains, NY: Peter Pauper Press.

Freedman, R. (1987). *Lincoln: A photobiography.* New York: Houghton Mifflin.

Gardner, H. (1994). *Creating minds: An anatomy of creativity seen through the lives of Freud, Einstein, Picasso, Stravinsky, Eliot, Graham, and Gandhi.* New York: Basic Books.

Gardner, H. (2006). *Multiple intelligences: New horizons.* New York: Perseus.

Grigorenko, E. L., Jarvin, L., & Sternberg, R. J. (2002). School-based tests of the triarchic theory of human intelligence: Three settings, three samples, three syllabi. *Contemporary Educational Psychology, 27,* 167–208.

Lee, H. (1960). *To kill a mockingbird.* New York: Warner Books.

Marzano, R. J., Pickering, D. J., & Pollock, J. F. (2004). *Classroom instruction that works: Research-based strategies for increasing student achievement.* Alexandria, VA: Association for Supervision and Curriculum Development.

Sternberg, R. J., Ferrari, M., Clinkenbeard, R. P., & Grigorenko, E. L. (1996). Identification, instruction, and assessment of gifted children: A construct validation of a triarchic model. *Gifted Child Quarterly, 40,* 129–137.

Sternberg, R. J., & Grigorenko, E. L. (2007). *Teaching for successful intelligence* (2nd ed.). Thousand Oaks, CA: Corwin Press.

Sternberg, R. J., Grigorenko, E. L., & Jarvin, L. (2001). Improving reading instruction: The triarchic model. *Educational Leadership, 58*(6), 48–52.

Sternberg, R. J., Torff, B., & Grigorenko, E. L. (1998). Teaching for successful intelligence raises school achievement. *Phi Delta Kappan 79,* 667–669.

Taba, H. (1962). *Curriculum development: Theory and practice.* Orlando, FL: Harcourt Publishing.

Tyler, R. W. (1949). *Basic principles of curriculum and instruction*. Chicago: University of Chicago Press.

Wells, H. G. (1988). *The island of Dr. Moreau* (Rev. ed.). New York: Penguin.

Index